AMERICA by MOTORCYCLE

In memory of Ma

AMERICA by MOTORCYCLE

Gary P. Stockbridge

iUniverse, Inc.
New York   Bloomington

America by Motorcycle

The views expressed in this work are solely those of the author and do not necessarily reflect the views of the publisher, and the publisher hereby disclaims any responsibility for them.

iUniverse books may be ordered through booksellers or by contacting:

iUniverse
1663 Liberty Drive
Bloomington, IN 47403
www.iuniverse.com
1-800-Authors (1-800-288-4677)

Because of the dynamic nature of the Internet, any Web addresses or links contained in this book may have changed since publication and may no longer be valid.

ISBN: 978-1-4401-9307-1 (sc)
ISBN: 978-1-4401-9308-8 (ebk)

Printed in the United States of America

iUniverse rev. date: 1/18/2010

Contents

Introduction

When I drove across the country in 1990. I kept a notebook, and I kept every bit of literature that I received at the National Parks. I took over 500 photographs and put them in my photo albums, in the correct order. I didn't have any intention of ever writing about my experience. I just wanted to remember as much as I possibly could.

While writing the parts of this book that involve my family, I tried to be careful not to hurt anybody's feelings. But, at the same time, this is my view of events, and everybody has their own opinions. I didn't sugar coat it.

I hope the only people that read it are the ones with an open mind, and heart. Everything that I have written is factually accurate and true. If there are any mistakes, they are honest mistakes. So, to the cynics I say, go away, you won't like it. But, if you have an open mind, and you are not judgemental then I think you will like it. Anyway, I did my best, and after all is said and done. I am a printer. I am not a writer.

In 2002 I started to have health problems and my vision deteriorated to 20/100, and glasses didn't help. I had lost all my peripheral vision, and I was no longer able to differentiate between certain colors. Red and green looked the same.

I was fired from numerous jobs, due to quality issues. Being a printer by trade, excellent vision is crucial to success. I was getting hired for jobs, but I knew it was only a matter of time. My resume from 2002 to 2010 is practically unusable, because of lost jobs due to health issues.

I started writing to try and do something positive with all my free time, and I was afraid I may go blind, and I wanted to write things down. It was very difficult to do. The type was fuzzy and I had to strain to read the screen.

To fill out the text, and to be more accurate in my account. I did a lot of research about all the places I saw, and didn't see, but were along my route. Hopefully, by doing this I could learn, and if anyone ever read it, then they could learn, and could potentially see what I saw, or what I missed. I hope this information is not boring to you, or it doesn't seem like filler.

A couple of the chapters were written as a diary, on the day that things happened. The chapter about my ride down to Gloucester, and the chapter when I went for an M.R.I., and when I was waiting for the results, were written this way. I then changed them slightly while editing so they read in the past tense.

I love this country, and I love my family, I hope this comes through. I am grateful for the life I have led, and the family relationships, even if many of these relationships are strained or broken. I have a lot of good memories. I'm not bitter, I'm thankful.

I hope any family that goes through what we did in my family, realizes that a person can still have a worthwhile and satisfying life, and enjoy many of the gifts that life has to offer, even after a stroke, and even with a feeding tube. I know my mother was thankful for the extra time she was given, despite the enormous challenges she faced.

I did not write a word for years. I found myself in the position of being the primary person that my mother depended on, and the person that made sure my mother's daily needs were met. For doing this, I found myself in the situation of having to defend myself constantly, from many in my own family. There were so many things said, that I could not *possibly prove wrong*, or could I *prove* the contents of my heart. But, my mother knew, and that was sufficient for me. I just hope and pray that someday, the family members that misjudged me, realize this mistake. God Bless you all.

Chapter One

NoW Or Never

That's it! I've had it! I quit! With that, I walked outside, got on my bike and went home. It was Late May 1990. I was living in two rooms on the third floor of a shared Apartment in Lexington, Massachusetts. Four of us, and an Airedale named Ina. This had played out before in my life. I have had more jobs than I could possibly count. I never worried much about finding another one, and I usually ended up making more money than the previous one. Quitting can feel very good, very freeing, especially if your boss is a jerk.

This time in particular felt very good. I arrived for work one morning and my boss was waiting for me. But, instead of calling me to his office, he berated me in front of my co-worker's. I had printed a job the day before that was sticking together. It could of been for several reason's, but I didn't stick around to figure it out. I told him where to go, and what he could do with the job, in front of my co-worker's. I *may* have used some profanity.

The wheels in my head were turning, and they wouldn't stop. I always wanted to see the country, and I was thinking this might be my best chance. I had $3,000 in the bank. The bike was almost new, but needed tires. So, I bought tires. I started making a list of what I would like to have with me, and fine tuned it to the bare essentials.

There were a couple of babies about to be born, and I was feeling a little guilty about leaving. My brother Scott and his wife Michele were due any day, and my brother David and his wife Ellen were due shortly after. I wanted to stay, but I felt I had to go. I stayed until Cassie and Raisa were born on June 7th, and the 14th, respectively, and then I left on June 16th. Cassie is my brother Scott's daughter and Raisa is my brother David's. I am their Uncle Gary, and Cassie is my Godchild. I am also the Godfather of my brother Richard's daughter. Her name is Kate.

I could hardly sleep the night before, and with the first hint of light, I was loading the bike. Off I went, to where I didn't know but I was going south. My nerves were jumping and I was driving too fast. I almost dumped my bike while making my first highway change.

My first night on the road I camped at a KOA campground in Pennsylvania. The trees were stripped almost bare from the Gypsy moths. Their incessant knawing and their droppings on my tent sounded like rain. I dreamed they were eating through my tent. The morning couldn't come soon enough.

I had been studying my maps and decided to take Route 50. George Washington mapped this road. There is a sign in Ocean city, Maryland that reads,"Sacramento 3073 miles". This is basically

America's Main street. It came before any other thoroughfare. I would find that this road will take you down the Main street, in the center of any town that it passed through. This route traces most of the Pioneer trails. This is the way I wanted to see America. On the back roads.

It was a beautiful day for a ride. I got on to route 50, and started the ride with long, gradual, sweeping turns that weaved their way through the hills and valleys. There was no-one on the road but me, it seemed. Upon entering West Virginia I noticed the homes were very poor. Small, run down homes dotted the hillside and it seemed that for every house there were two junk cars in the yard. I felt bad for these people, and their situation, but by the looks I got from a couple of locals I felt that I should just keep moving. I do think that it is a beautiful place to see, and the roads are as twisty as any in the country, but I don't think I would want to live there.

Entering Ohio, the road straightened out a lot. It was very rural with long distances between towns. Many of the barns had faded ads of "Mail Pouch Tobacco" painted on their sides. The painted advertisements looked over 25 years old, some barely readable. The long rolling hills combined with the fresh air, the smell of summer, and the sound of my bike, soothed my mind like summer rain on the cottage roof.

1986 KAWASAKI CONCOURS 1000

The one thing that almost all my motorcycle trips have in common, is that they are preceded by the feeling that I have to go. The printing business, and operating printing machinery, on deadlines, may have something to do with this. The solvents and inks can put you in a haze after a while. At least it did that to me. But, once I'm out on the road, it all starts to clear up. I feel like the sun is just burning up the fog in my mind. I just start to soak it in, and realize how good life is. The sights, sounds and the riding combined are good for the head. For me it's not about the motorcycle, as it is the ride. This trip was on a 1986 Kawasaki Concours, 1000 cc., sport tourer. It was designed for travel but the engine was the same as the Ninja. It was incredibly powerful (100 horsepower), and fast. This bike was perfectly suited for this trip, and was as reliable as a Timex watch.

It seemed the further I got from home, the better I felt, and the anticipation of what was ahead, made me anxious to press on. Then I got to Cincinnati. It was 100 degrees in the shade. Which there was none. The city was run down. The roads were rough and the smell of industry was heavy in the air. The traffic was very heavy, and I was hot, tired, and ready to stop. I rode on until Versailles, Indiana, and found a motel in Larry Bird's "back yard". Larry is my favorite athlete, and he brought my hometown Boston Celtics three championships in the eighties. Larry is from French Lick. The next town over. He had a bar nearby, but I never made it. I was toast.

It rained overnight and into the morning. This was good. It cooled the air and made me eager to move on. So much to see. I stayed on route 50, which took me through Hoosier National Forest. It had long sweeping turns and a great smooth road, as well as scenery. It was smooth sailing. After leaving the forest the sun was beginning to set with an orange glow. There were gas wells pumping throughout the area, with the yellow light of a flame on each one.

Then I entered Missouri. I had no idea where I was going to stay, and looking at my map at the Dairy Queen over dinner, I thought about St. Louis. Now it was dark, and I was 50 miles from there. Going in to St. Louis, with no idea where I was going, caused me some concern. East St. Louis at night is not where you would want to get lost. I found a Youth Hostel with no problem, and checked in. There were six others there. Four men and two women. Three from Germany, one from Switzerland, and two from N.Y.. We bought some beer and watched the fireworks over the Mississippi river until 2a.m.

Wednesday morning, June 19, time to get up. I hate to say it but I wish I didn't drink so many beers. My head was throbbing and my whole body ached. It was going to be hot as hell out there today, so I figured the earlier the better to hit the road. I ate breakfast, did my chore as required (wash shower), said goodbye and left. I checked out the St. Louis Arch before leaving St. Louis.

I chose I-70 for the sake of making some time. I rode over 200 miles, hung-over. What a day. It seemed like all I did, all day, was read billboards. I was wiped out and decided to stop 20 miles east of Kansas City. I found a $14.00 a night motel with a t.v that had an orange picture, and a sunken bed. It was a good time to stop. There was a tornado watch in effect. I walked to the Pizza Hut for a bowl of spaghetti, then went home and called it a day.

The day before had taught me that I-70 will bore you to numbness. I got back on Rt. 50. This was starting out to be a great day. The weather was good and the roads were like long meandering ribbons across the plains. It was hot, but that was to be expected. The traffic? What traffic? It was just me and an occasional tractor or pickup. But cows. I've never seen so many cows, feed lots and cows. I must of seen a million (?) head of cattle that day. Not to mention the smell. I remember thinking that if they could get cow flatulence in a can, it could solve our energy problems.

I stopped to take a couple of pictures, and met three couples on their way to New Mexico. They were riding Yamaha Venture Royales. We talked for a little while and then we split up. I went into Dodge City and checked into the Thunderbird motel. I checked out 10 minutes later, reasoning that I would rather sleep on the ground than at that shithole. There was a campground not too far back, so I turned around. I checked in, and as I was setting up my tent, I hear "hey Boston, want a beer?" It was the people from the feedlot. They asked if I wanted to go out for cocktails, and I did. It was a good dinner and the first real conversation in a while. There was a wet T-shirt contest in the next room. When we were leaving I saw one girl outside topless but she couldn't of been the winner. My new friends were going back to the campground, but I wasn't quite ready, so we said goodnight, and I went for a ride.

The night was still young and I was a little too revved up to go lie in my tent, and I didn't want to impose on my neighbors. So, I rode around Boot Hill and tried to imagine what it was like back when there were gunfighters, saloons, and horses in the street. I visited the Boot Hill graveyard, but I didn't see any names I recognized.

I found a bar and went in. There were four pool tables, and all were busy. There were a lot of people inside, mostly Mexicans. We were a long way from Mexico but they must come here for the work. I challenged one table and won a few games before I retired to a bar stool and asked for a beer. "Where you from? Boston?" my bar mate to my right asked. "What brings you to Dodge? "Just Passing Through", was my reply. So, me and my new friend who introduced himself as "The Mayor of Dodge City" sat there and talked and drank until we closed the place. Now.... I was ready to go to sleep.

The sun rose at what seemed like hours early the next day. I took advantage of it. I got up, showered, did my laundry, ate breakfast, had a few cups of coffee, and packed up by 7:30. I got some advice from the store owner on what there was to see in the area, and asked him about route 50 west. "Long and Lonely" was his reply. Turns out route 50 has the distinction of being named "The loneliest highway in America." I sat by the pool for a while and thought about what was ahead. Kansas is 500 miles across and I had already ridden about 300. It was hard to believe but I was only five days in to this ride and I had a pocket full of cash and no particular place to go, but west. It felt good.

My new friends from the night before began to get up one by one and get themselves going. We said our goodbyes and good lucks and I was on my way. I remember feeling both happy and sad at the same time. I just met these people but I was going to miss them, and this town.

I never expected what I was about to see on the plains of Kansas. Wild donkeys, mule deer watching from the distance, and an occasional coyote. The road was just as straight as an arrow as far as you could see, with nothing on either side, and the mountains were hundreds of miles in front of me. It was something to see and nothing to see at the same time. Route 50 parallels the old "Sante Fe Trail" almost exactly. The Sante Fe Trail was used between 1820 and 1880 by traders until the railroads were first completed. The peak was during the civil war when 5,000 wagons would be making the 750 mile long trip at one time. There are a lot of roadside plaques if you have the time to stop and read them, and small remnants of the trail can still be found.

The man back at the campground told me," You shouldn't miss The Great Sand Dunes" and he was right. It was mind boggling when I came upon it. The sand apparently moves around depending on the wind but always stays together. The sheer size of these dunes was staggering. Me and my motorcycle would be nothing more than a speck in comparison.

It was H-O-T. 110 degrees in the shade. Keeping myself from burning up or dehydrating was becoming a challenge. I traveled at over one hundred miles an hour for an hour and a half and saw practically no-one. I was beginning to worry just a little. I saw vultures circling above and I didn't want to be their dinner.

The landscape after entering Colorado on route 50 was very much like Kansas. It was just flat agricultural prairie as far as you could see. Many of the towns along this road had a water tower with the town's name painted on it. There were a lot of farms and ranches, but the lifeblood of Colorado is outdoor recreation. But, that is still up ahead.

The Rockies were now in front of me, and what a sight. The land gradually began to change to alpine meadows and the farms and flatland disappeared into my mirror. The Rockies began to rise in front of me as the road gradually took me up through the rugged canyons. Then the mountains were beginning to surround me on three sides. The road was beginning to climb steeper and I soon would be crossing the Continental Divide. The air temperature began to drop. It started at 100 degrees and then 90, 80, and when I was approaching the top it was 70 degrees. This was awesome as far as motorcycling goes. The weather was perfect, the scenery was amazing, and the bike was running great. When I reached the top it was 13,272 feet. WOW! What a day! It was time for rest.

Chapter Two

San Juan Skyway

Rest I wanted, but would I get comfort. The less money I spent on lodging, the further I could go. I was checking out the rates at a motel when I was approached by this Harley, Biker type guy, with a long beard and huge belly. "Isn't that uncomfortable, riding bent over like that?" he asked me. " Not too bad", was my reply. "Is the San Juan Skyway worth checking out?", I asked him. "Absolutely, We're riding it tomorrow, you can ride it with us if you want". We agreed to meet there at 7:a.m. His name was Dave.

I decided to camp out. It was hot and dry, and the campground was in the desert. The couple in the camp next to me invited me for a franks and beans dinner, and wine. I accepted. They were fulfilling a lifelong dream of driving across the U.S. together. They were on a big Goldwing. They were 65 years old. The coyotes were howling, and I was convinced that there was one outside my tent that night, But the wind was blowing and there were shadows, so I'm not sure.

As I was packing up at 6: a.m. my new friend poked his head out and wished me luck. I arrived at the motel right on time to meet Dave and co. but these guys weren't close to ready. It turns out it was Dave, Dan, and his son, Darren. Dan was a real character, he kept us laughing. He was kind of short, bald, mid- forties. Darren was 13, a real cool kid, He was wearing snakeskin boots, and all the right gear for motorcycling. We hit it off right away. Kids and dogs almost always like me. I'm grateful for that since I love kids and dogs.

These guys had done this ride before. The San Juan Skyway is a 236 mile loop through the southwest corner of Colorado. I had no idea the treat, and thrill I was in for. We planned ahead to stop for breakfast in Telluride and we were on our way. It was beautiful from the start, and the roads were perfect as we climbed up into the mountains. It was about 50 degrees with scattered showers.

The scenery reminded me of Switzerland (from photos), with the snow tipped mountains, deep blue lakes, and waterfalls around almost every turn. These guys were riding fast and I was having a hard time keeping up. I almost lost control in a hard turn on wet pavement. My front wheel slid sideways and put me across the center line (luckily no-one was coming), before I got it under control and eased it back. I slowed down after that. I didn't want my bike being shipped home, or me for that matter. The breakfast was good in Telluride and we moved on through old mining towns that had long since been abandoned. I looked through the window of one old store and the calendar was from 1960. It looked like everything was just left in place and deserted.

DURANGO & SILVERTON RAILROAD

We stopped for a burger and a couple of beers in Silverton. The ride then brought us past old deserted mines, and the ecological evidence of mining on the mountains. Where there was once mining, there was now just bright orange soil, and large sections of ruined forest.

Our next stop was Durango. We had dinner and checked into a motel. After lounging around the pool for a few cocktails we started to settle in. I got the cot. They didn't want any money but I insisted, and chipped in $20.00.

The next morning we were talking about our plans, and they asked me if I wanted to join them on their trip to Taos, New Mexico. It sounded like it would be a lot of fun, and I appreciated the offer, but I wanted to keep going west to California. It was kind of sad leaving these guys, it was a great couple of days.

Next stop, Mesa Verde National Park and Indian ruins from 500 b.c.. It was over 110 degrees, so I didn't stay long. Then I traveled through Ute indian reservation. These people are poor beyond belief. They lived in very small dwellings that appeared to be made of cement. They had what appeared to be outhouses next to them. There is no shade out there, and it looked like they didn't have a/c., or indoor bathrooms. The state of Utah is named for the Utes. It was in this area that I saw wild horses roaming free.

Then I entered Arizona. I never expected it to be so beautiful. The rock formations from the wind and sand were amazing. The rocks were vivid shades of browns, oranges, reds, and yellows. When the sun was setting on these rocks, I didn't want to leave because the colors kept changing. I stopped for the night just before sunset.

The following day was the same routine, get up early, shower, pack, and double-check everything. I knew this day would be hot, arid, parched, and lonely. This is Navajo country. Their reservation was huge. It took me a day to drive across it. I found a motel just off the reservation at sunset. I had a cold beer and a cold shower after checking in. That was the hottest day yet. 115 degrees. I was baked.

Chapter Three

Grand Canyon and Zion

That was a good motel. It had a restaurant, ice cold a/c., cold bottled beer, and most of all a great bed. This was a good opportunity to get some rest, study my maps and think a little bit of how far I had come, and where I was going. I had been driving across Indian reservations for the last two days and the Grand Canyon was ahead. The weather forecast was calling for a heat wave under bright sunny skies, with highs of 115 degrees. So, on my bike, with my leather jacket, gloves and long pants, I knew it would be difficult. I had to wear all that gear so I wouldn't burn. All day long I had to keep putting sun block on my face.

I had been on the road for eight days, and had covered about 300 miles a day. This may not seem like a lot but I would start at about seven a.m., and stop at sunset most days. I allowed time to see the sights, but sometimes I felt a little like Chevy Chase in National Lampoon Vacation. I would stop, look, get on my bike and go. The road ahead was always more intriguing to me than where I was.

The Grand Canyon was a couple of hours ahead. I decided to go to the north rim, because there were less tourists, and it was north, which is the direction I wanted to start heading. The heat was starting to get to me a bit and I was looking forward to the California coast.

As I got closer to the North Rim entrance, the road began to rise and trees began to appear. The air began to cool and and there was now some shade. The higher I went, the more trees there were, until finally I was driving this winding road through a forest. There were meadows, and deer, and wild flowers in bloom. I then came to a fork in the road, and there were vehicles going one way and none the other, and that's the one I took.

After about 20 minutes on this road I got my first view of the canyon. It was GRAND. But seriously, it is an amazing thing to see, and no photograph or movie could ever begin to translate what this is. Just the thought of the Colorado river carving this canyon was astonishing. I went right out on the edge of the cliff and sat there by myself for an hour and a half. Then I had to get moving.

THE GRAND CANYON

I quickly regretted leaving so soon. The air was a scorching heat, blasted into my face. My eyes were as dry as a bone and they were as red as hell. The landscape was barren.

After entering Utah I saw one solitary tree, and a patch of grass, that seemed like a mirage at first. But, it was real. I stopped and sat for a good while until another traveler stopped and gave me a drink of cold water. The one thing this trip is doing for me, more than anything, is showing me the kindness of strangers.

I came to a fork in the road, and I stopped to look at my map. One way was Bryce Canyon and one way was Zion National park. I chose Zion. It was the right choice. This park is a jewel. This is a small park, but gorgeous, with it's high orange cliffs, and ice cold, crystal clear rivers. It was an oasis on the desert. I went for a swim in the Virgin river. The most refreshing and needed swim of my life. I have to thank God for how good things are going, and you can't help but think of creation when you see things like this.

ZION NATIONAL PARK

I had a few hours of sun left when I decided to start riding again. At 9:p.m. I found a twenty dollar a night motel and stopped. Tomorrow Nevada.

Wednesday, June 26. I knew this was going to be my longest and hottest day. I would be crossing the desert just north of Death Valley, so you get the idea. I ate breakfast and started riding when I began to worry about gas. My gas tank is seven gallons, I had less than a half tank, and it was 110 miles to Tonapah, Nevada, and the next available fuel. I made it by the slightest of margins. I had run my reserve, and literally ended up sputtering into town. I always topped off after this.

This stretch of road is something else. It's perfectly straight as far as you can see. The Sierra Nevada mountains were off in the distance. The signs were all shot up. There were burro's and bulls walking right out on the road, and tumbleweeds moving around with the wind, just like the movies.

I got my first speeding ticket of the ride for doing 125 miles an hour on this road. A motorcycle cop was hiding behind a bush. This guy was the homeliest son of a bitch you would ever see. He looked kind of like Jim Carey in Me Myself and Irene in the scene when he's riding the motorcycle with the bugs in his teeth. He didn't have bugs in his teeth but they were big, widely spaced chiclets. I asked about the signs and he flashed a big smile and said, "this is the wild west boy". There was a fight and gunshots outside my motel that night. I looked out my curtains numerous times to see what the hell was going on, and to check on my bike. Tomorrow, California. Thank god! I've had enough of Nevada!

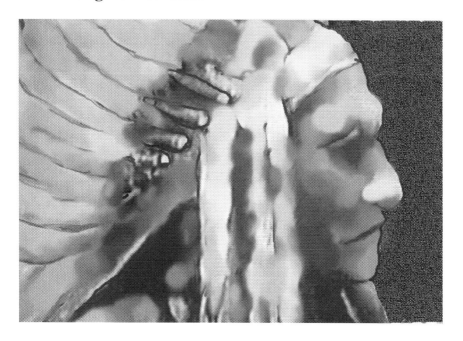

INDIAN CHIEF

Chapter Four

The West Coast

California bound. It was early in the morning and the weather was fine. The Sierra Nevada mountains were now right in front of me. I crossed the mountains and entered into California that morning. What struck me most about these mountains, was that it was desert on one side, and lush forest on the other. The mountains seemed to act as a squeegee and take the moisture out of the clouds coming off the Pacific. This was a great ride. The road took long sweeping turns through a great forest and led me right into Yosemite National Park. This was the first time I ran into a lot of tourists and probably would have enjoyed it more midweek. But regardless, it was something to see. There were lakes and waterfalls and wildlife, but the trees, that's what really affected me. Some over 2000 years old. So big it would take ten men, hand to hand to reach around. So dense and high that only trickles of sun would reach the forest floor. Seeing these trees alone made this trip worth while for me.

After leaving Yosemite I stopped for gas and a cold drink. The store was on a bend in the road, and I was sitting on the stairs eating some chocolate chip cookies and drinking a quart of gatorade when I heard an unmistakable noise. Harley Davidsons. At least twenty with straight pipes. As they came around the bend, several looked my way as I sat next to my bike (rice-burner), and then they all started giving me the finger. Including one biker mama. As they went passed I noticed it was the Hells Angels. I didn't respond to their gestures but I did see them later. We ended up eating breakfast at the same restaurant. I sat at the counter right next to these guys. I did leave some space between my bike and theirs though. I didn't want to take any chances. My bike was fine when I left.

It was getting to be late afternoon so I started to think about stopping. I looked in my guide book and saw that there was a K.O.A. campground not too far ahead. I checked in, set up my tent, took a dip in the pool, and did my laundry. Later on I bought some beer and sat by the pool reading "The Catcher in The Rye"until a busload of Europeans arrived. I stopped reading and just let them entertain me for awhile. At about 9 p.m. I called it a day and went to sleep.

The following morning was another beauty. I took my time getting up, and I listened to some some old time religion on my radio for awhile before breaking down my tent and packing up my stuff. It was Sunday morning, and when I finally got going it seemed like I had the road to myself. The California landscape was very distinctive in this area with it's rolling hills and valleys. It then changed to vineyards and farms, and then eventually began to get more congested as I approached the ocean.

The Pacific ocean. I was finally there, and it was so blue. I had taken the scenic route and had driven 5,000 miles at this point. I went to the shore and soaked in the scenery for a while, and did some girl watching. There were a lot of beautiful girls on the beach.

San Francisco was my next stop. I checked out Fisherman's wharf and drove around the whole city. There was a youth hostel just outside the city, but unfortunately it was full. So, I relaxed down by the water for awhile, watched the people, and took pictures of the row houses. Then I headed over to the Golden Gate Bridge Park. I did the tourist thing again, took some pictures, ate lunch, and then drove across the bridge. It was pretty exciting and the weather was great.

As soon as you cross the bridge the landscape changes. This is route 1. The road was very narrow and very winding as it hugged the coast. I passed through the Golden Gate National Recreation Area and then the road went inland for awhile. I took a small detour at Point Reyes National Seashore and checked out the Point Reyes Lighthouse. The lighthouse is a long way down, to stay below the fog. It looked like a few too many steps for me. So, I just took a picture. This would be a great place to spend a day. The locals say that seeing whales from here is common. Route 1 then went through small towns, and weaved through the valleys, and took me along the cliffs on the shore. I passed one beautiful beach after another. The fog rolled in and then out again and the temperature would go from 80 to 65.

I would pass through Bodega Bay. Alfred Hitchcocks, "The Birds" was filmed here. I stopped and rented a cabin in Manchester right on the beach. There was no T.V. or running water. Just a wooden bed with a two inch thick mattress. It was exactly what I wanted. I was exhausted. I decided to spend two nights there. I had the campground almost to myself. The shore was deserted, and I saw two great sunsets, and wild deer and jackrabbits down by the beach. I called my mother from here and she was very happy to hear from me. My mother's name is Eunice. I call her Ma.

I finished The Catcher In The Rye, got a great night sleep, and was up early to get going. Those two days felt like a mini vacation and I felt re-energized. I had only traveled about 100 miles in California at this point. I wanted to take my time. The next 100 miles of route 1 was right on the coast and it was perfect motorcycling. Heaven on hot-top. What struck me as so unique about the west coast were the sharp spires of rocks that are all shapes and sizes, just off shore. They call them sea stacks. They are quite far out into the ocean and are all unique. I would find out later that rocks like these have torn many ships to pieces.

The fog rolled in and out, and the mist hung along the shore. There seemed to be no-one on these beaches. I remember thinking at the time that the people here are so lucky. I couldn't imagine a better commute to work than down a road like this. Why did I think about *&^%$#@ Work?

The road was about to head inland, so I decided to look for a place to stay. I found one and pitched my tent. There was one person there that had been traveling around the country for over a year. I assume he was wealthy. The campground had no amenities whatsoever, but there was a restaurant nearby, so I cleaned up and had dinner there. I had a prime rib with baked potato and french onion soup. After dinner I had a few drinks at the bar, watched t.v., and talked to the bartender. I was the only one at the bar. I slept good, but the ground was hard and bumpy.

The following morning started out very cool. It was 45 or 50 degrees, with fog. By midmorning it was burning off, and I stopped for "brunch" in a restaurant I had no business being in. The "clientele" wore suits and dresses and they had a piano player "noodling" on the keys. So, this is how the other half lives? They can keep it. I'll take a diner any day. But they let me in and I was hungry.

It turned out to be a great day for riding. The road took it's sweet time passing vineyards and farms, and winding it's way through the hills for the next 70 miles or so. This was my fourth day in California. I was now on 101 and the road and the riding were great. The next time I would see the ocean, would be in Eureka. I did take one detour off of rt.101 to ride "The Avenue of the Giants". This is a 30 mile ride through a redwood forest on old 101. The road is surrounded by Humboldt Redwoods State Park, and goes along the Eel river. The park contains the largest virgin stand of redwoods in the world. One tree in this forest, named "The Dyerville Giant" is over 362 feet tall, and 52 feet around. I got off my bike and spent some time among these trees in total solitude. This place seemed sacred and I remember thinking that some of these trees were here when Jesus was last seen.

On to Crescent City. A very ordinary, working class town. It was cool and damp when I arrived there, so I stopped for a cup of coffee and a bowl of chowder. I noticed old photos on the wall, of destruction, and I asked about them. On March 27, 1964, there was an 8.4 earthquake in Alaska. This created a tsunami, or tidal wave, 50 feet in height. The first two waves struck at low tide and did little damage and killed only one person. The next two waves killed 11 people in Crescent City and 110 people total, from Alaska to California.

I would learn later while researching this, about another tragic event that happened on July 28,1865. In San Francisco, The Brother Jonathan, a 220 foot ship with two decks, was loaded with over 850 tons of cargo. The captain, Captain DeWolf noticed the ship getting too low in the water and told the company's agent to stop loading. The agent refused, and went ahead and loaded a three stamp ore crusher that weighed over three tons. The weather was getting bad and the 244 passengers were beginning to board the ship. When the ship tried to leave it wouldn't budge and they had to be pulled out with a tug.

The Brothers Jonathan off-loaded some cargo in Crescent City and was once again under way. The weather was getting worse and they weren't making any headway. The captain decided to turn back to

Crescent City to wait out the storm. The course he chose showed no obstructions on the maps.

When a shipmate was going to ready the anchor he noticed a rock and yelled. But, it was too late. The waves heaved the ship up and dropped it on a 250 foot pinnacle of rock rising up from the ocean floor. The ship was being broken up on the rock and was sinking. The Captain ordered everyone to save themselves. Not many did. Only 19 people, of the 244 aboard, survived. For several weeks the bodies and wreckage came ashore. The rock was named Jonathan Rock. The Brother's Johnathan was discovered in 1993 loaded with a bounty of gold and treasure.

CALIFORNIA COAST

REDWOODS

That night I stayed at a Youth hostel in the Redwood National Forest in Klamath Oregon. I shared a room with four others and we had a view of the ocean. After settling in I took a ride, I found a road very close to the shore with thick bushes and small trees on both sides. The sun was about to set, and the sky was oranges and pinks. I almost couldn't ride my bike any slower, maybe five m.p.h. I was just soaking in the sights and sounds, when a big cat came out in front of me. Fifteen feet in front of me at the most. It was in the air when it appeared . It's feet touched the ground once, and it was gone to my left. It never looked directly at me, that I saw. It looked to be about sixty pounds, It had a short-ish tail, with a dark-ish coat. There were tufts behind the ears. It didn't make a sound. I think it was a Lynx. That was wild, and the coolest thing I have seen so far.

After that, I was wound up, and I went looking for a place to eat. I found a bar with a pool table. The waitress was very nice, very good looking, and fit. I had a burger and talked for a good long while with her. She told me about her life, the west, and especially the trees. She spoke with reverence of them and warned me about the destruction I would soon be seeing. Clear cutting in Oregon and Washington. After a few beers I had a good buzz, so I decided to head back to the hostel for the night. My house mates were still up and I hung out with them for awhile. I told them about the big cat that I saw, and described it. The consensus was that it was either a Lynx, or a cougar that was missing part of it's tail.

There was one guy that got on my nerves. He was a total bullshit artist in my opinion. He said he was in Panama during the invasion. He was in the middle of the big earthquake in California. He was near Mt. St. Helens when it blew. This guy never shut up. Not even when he was sleeping. He made more noise than the three stooges. Then the following morning he wanted to borrow my soap. Sorry pal. The people there were nice though. For seven dollars I got a bunk in an old house with an ocean view in a redwood forest.

CALIFORNIA CAT

The following morning I slept late, and then spent a couple of hours reading. Check out time was 11:00 and my chore was the shower. So, I waited until we were all done, I washed the shower, packed up and got ready to leave. In a short while I would be in Oregon. It was another great day for riding, and I was rested, and ready.

I entered Oregon on rt. 101 around 1:00. The route continued right along the shore. The Klamath mountains were to my right, and the rocky shore was to my left. There were high, jagged cliffs around every bend, with beautiful views, and wildflowers in bloom, everywhere.

There was more congestion, motels, and places to eat along this stretch of road. Which was fine, I was hungry. I was on this road for the whole day, and hundreds of miles, before I decided to start heading northeast towards Portland. There was a youth hostel a couple of hours ahead.

Any kind of building can be a youth hostel, and they are run by all types of people. Some are very clean and organized and others are not. This one was a ranch style home in the middle of the forest, with two rivers nearby. There were six of us there, and a black labrador retriever. We all pooled some money for food, and had a great dinner of salmon and potato. The salmon was caught by the owner in the river right out back. I stayed in that night and read. I was reading John Steinbeck's "Travels with Charley". It's about him and his dog driving around the country.

Chapter Five

Portland Oregon, Washington State, and Idaho

I got going early the next day and got to Portland around noon. I found the hostel, and then went to do my laundry. It was a cool, drizzly, overcast day. Check-in was 3:00. This was a home, right downtown, with bunk beds and a common shower. I met a couple of guys there and we decided to go drinking. One was from England, and one was from Australia. We decided to take public transportation downtown, and quickly found a sports bar, with a pooltable, and t.v.'s. We ordered some burgers and started playing pool. The Englishman wasn't so good, but the Aussie was very good. We were getting along really well, but the Aussie was enjoying his victories a little too much. He was rubbing it in to me and my new English friend. He began to get under my skin a bit, and I found myself getting very focused on the game, and I started shooting very well. By the end of the night he wasn't so boisterous. But we got along great, just a little friendly competition. The next day we all went to a blues festival and spent the whole day. I will say this about the Aussie. He could really drink.

Before leaving the Portland area, I decided to check out the Columbia River Gorge. I would ride a portion of it anyway. I joined several people from the Portland hostel. They went in a jeep and I rode my bike. This is a beautiful area. It has mountains, the Columbia river, and many waterfalls. The people I went with knew some of the better things to see. You could easily spend a week or more in this area. Leaving Portland, I rode through some light rain. I was still heading north towards Mt. St. Helens. I knew this was going to be something to see, and I couldn't wait to get there. I then entered the state of Washington.

It had been almost 10 years since the eruption. It was precipitated by a 5.1 earthquake, the north face of Mt. St. Helens collapsed, in a massive Avalanche. In just a few moments, this massive slab of rock and debris slammed into Spirit lake. The debris and water then crossed a 1,300 foot ridge and continued 14 miles down the Toutle river.

The explosion itself, released a gas and rock filled wind, that swept down across the ridges and forest. One hundred and fifty square miles of forest was blown over, or left dead. It also created a mushroom shaped column of ash, that rose thousands of feet skyward, and the drifting ash turned day into night. I spoke with a woman two towns away. She told me birds were smashing into their windows trying to escape it. The eruption lasted nine hours.

To see this desolate, destroyed place, was un-describable. But, still you could see new trees poking through to start again. I hope to go back there some day.

MULTNOMAH FALLS

MOUNT SAINT HELENS

MOUNT ST. HELENS AREA DESTRUCTION

I got on route 5, and started heading straight north towards Seattle. This was a "making time" road. I decided I would take route 5 to route 101, which encompasses the entire Olympic National Park. I picked up 101 in Olympia and started north towards Port Townsend. The Puget Sound and Seattle were to my right, but not visible to me. There was water to my right, and mountains on my left. The water was an inlet to Puget.

The first thing I noticed upon entering this area were the logging trucks, one after the other. This surprised me because I didn't think there would be logging in a national park.

I stopped in Port Angeles for a bite to eat, and one young girl got my attention. She was about 16. Her job was to wear a sign board that covered her front and back. She kept walking back and forth in front of a restaurant, and very unenthusiastically would announce the special. She was very cute, and very friendly, but she did not want her picture taken. She was too embarrassed.

Unfortunately, as nice as this area is. Logging rules. This is their life, and their living in this area. I would soon find out that criticism is not well received. The trucks rolled on, all day long, and they were stacked incredibly high. The noise, and smell, and the heat kept my nerves on edge. There are a lot of roads off route 101 and out to the shore, and I checked a lot of them out. The rocky cliffs and wildness seemed to take me back, imagining North America before the United States of America. There was very little development right on the coast from what I saw. The Makah Indian Reservation is at the northwest tip of Olympia. I stood on the shore, and just soaked in the fact that there wasn't a soul in sight, in any direction.

I first saw clear- cutting in Oregon, and there was much more up here. Clear- cutting is basically just what it sounds like. They leave nothing. The animals. The trees. The whole area is just scraped clean. They do leave a "Sign" though. It states the company that did this, and they proclaim that this site is managed by. That kills me, "managed by"? To me this is rape of the environment. On more than one occasion I would say something to a local, and one guy told me to go back east and take a look at Maine before I criticize them.

I checked out Hoh rainforest in Olympic National Park. This is a temperate rain forest, and it is protected. Temperate rain forests are only found in New Zealand, southern Chile, and here. The rain here averages 145 inches a year. The dominant species of trees are Spruce, Hemlock, Douglas fir, Western Red Cedar, and Black Cottonwood. Some of these trees are three hundred feet high, and 23 feet in circumference. Entering this place was like going back in time, totally unspoiled virgin growth, with massive trees, and a forest floor with ancient fallen trees, There were long strands of moss, growing, and hanging from all the branches. Absolutely beautiful. Unfortunately there is just a small fraction left from it's original size.

As much as I liked this area, and the Olympic National Park especially, in the end, I was disappointed by what I saw. But, I've been in the printing business all of my adult life and I make my living using paper. So, my living depends on paper, and it's affordability for the customer. The thing that bothers me the most is that Japan is getting a very large share of this wood.

" Any fool can destroy trees. They can not run away, and if they could, they would still be destroyed, chased and hunted down as long as fun and a dollar could be got out of their bark hides, branching horns, or magnificent bole backbones. Few that fell trees, plant them, nor would planting avail much toward getting anything like the noble primeval forests. During a man's life only saplings can be grown, in the place of the old trees, tens of centuries old, that have been destroyed. It took more than three thousand years for some of the trees in these western woods, trees that still stand in perfect strength and beauty, waving and singing in the mighty forests of the Sierra. Through all the wonderful, eventful centuries since Christ's time, and long before that, God has cared for these trees, saved them from drought, disease, avalanches, and a thousand straining, leveling tempests and floods, but he can not save them from fools, only Uncle Sam can do that". John Muir from "Our National Parks," 1901.

I spent two days here, one of them in an old military base. It was the same place that "An Officer and a Gentleman", was filmed. I gave serious consideration at this point to go to Vancouver, British Columbia, but I decided to start heading east and took the ferry out of Port Townsend across the Puget Sound to Whidby island. This put me on route 20, Idaho. This road would take me through the North Cascades National Park. Absolutely gorgeous scenery, no traffic, and great weather. I have been very fortunate so far. I have not ridden in any significant rain at all. Everything is going great and I'm having the time of my life. I then started south on Route 155 towards the Grand Coulee Dam. I saw the effects of this dam long before I got to it. The land turned from dry and arid, to green, lush, farmland. The Apples I ate at roadside stands on this stretch of road were the best I ever had. I ate three in a row for lunch.

The Grand Coulee Dam irrigates up to a million acres, and the hydropower provides energy for a lot of homes, hospitals, hotels, factories, and schools. When I finally arrived at the dam I was immediately impressed with the sheer size, and the human accomplishment of a project this size. I spent an afternoon checking out the educational films, and the massive turbines and hydro-generators. Not to mention enjoying some cool air. Before leaving the area I met a couple on a motorcycle. The man was from Coer d'Alene Idaho. He said if I passed through there I could call him.

After a long but satisfying ride from The Grand Coulee dam, I found a campground in Hayden Lake, Idaho. It was early evening and I was tired and hungry. My campsite was all you could ask for. It was level, plenty of trees around, and it was up on the side of a hill. I set up my tent and had just finished a dinner of canned beans, when a neighbor arrived.

He looked harmless enough, medium build, unshaven, caucasian, greasy stringy hair, and clothes typical for a man camping in the woods. He resembled Gilligan (from Gilligan's island) somewhat. He was in a pickup truck, and alone. After noticing my license plate, he struck up a conversation. We began to talk. I had a small fire going by this time. It turned out he was from back east as well. After awhile, in the midst of casual conversation he used the word "nigger". I did not want to immediately become confrontational, after all, I was leaving in the morning. I did try to break off the conversation by saying I was going to go read for a while. But he just kept talking. Then he said it again. I corrected him as delicately as I could by responding that there are good and bad in all races, and that black people are no different.

He didn't like that, and his tone began to change. He was no longer just trying to get an idea about me. He was starting to spew hate with an angry tone. It turns out he was affiliated with the church of Jesus Christ Christian, a.k.a. the "Aryan nation". They were having their "United Congress" right down the road. They are white supremacists. I would later find out, that this is where they trained these racists, for urban terror and guerilla warfare.

I told him I was not a racist and did not share his views and I didn't want to hear any more. I put out the fire and went inside my tent. Now I was the enemy and he began focusing his angry words towards me. After I heard the words "Don't close your eyes". That was it, I packed my stuff in short order. I felt his eyes on me, but I didn't look at him. I got my money back for the camp and called my new friend from the Grand Coulee dam. He told me I could stay with him.

This was such a beautiful place, and these views are not shared by the regular folks that live here. But, it is a totally white population from what I saw and for this reason the Aryan Nation considers this it's "homeland". They believe the white race are the chosen ones.

What are the odds. I had driven thousands of miles and I ended up in a campsite next to a racist lunatic like this.

I drove to Lake C'or de'lene in C'or de'lene Idaho. What a beautiful lake and place. Now, I was among the affluent. The stately homes with their perfectly manicured lawns and almost unnatural perfection and uniformity. I felt out of place. I waited by the lake and watched the boats and people until my friend arrived to meet me.

He was with his son, Dan. Dan was about sixteen, and the old man, Matt, was about 45. We had dinner with all the extras at a very fancy restaurant, with white table linens, and a view of the lake. Which was great. The steak was great too. Matt insisted on paying for the meal, but he did let me get the tip.

We went back to his place, had a few beers, and looked through his telescope. I never saw stars that were brighter or clearer. This turned out to be a good day. I slept on the floor and left after breakfast the following morning.

Chapter Six

Montana and Wyoming

At this point I had been across the country the long way. I had reached the furthest distance from Massachusetts when I was in northwest Washington. I had been on the road for almost a month and I was averaging about 270 miles a day. I had traveled over 7,500 miles.

My body was beginning to feel the wear and tear of the road. In the beginning I could go hours without getting off the bike. But now I had to get off about every hour or so. My hips would get sharp pain from staying in the same position. My neck, shoulders, wrists, and knees were all feeling it. My bike needed an oil change. The rewards were great but the riding was beginning to feel a little bit like a job. Sunrise to sunset, every day, on the road.

I had to decide to keep heading east out of Idaho, and basically start heading home, or take a detour. I was tired, but I figured I may never be this way again so I decided to head north to Glacier / Waterton National Park. This park sits on both sides of the U.S. - Canadian border.

I left Idaho and started heading east across the Bitterroot Mountain Range of the Rocky mountains. I entered Montana and traveled about 100 miles before picking up route 93. I started heading north. It would be about 250 miles to get there.

This route would ride along the shore of the enormous Flathead lake. This lake was at least 30 miles long, and was in the Flathead Indian reservation. These Indians were perfectly normal, and please note their heads are no flatter than anyone else's.

My brother David had mentioned to me about the "Going To The Sun Road" in Glacier, and I was looking forward to driving it. I found a motel just west of the park and called it a day.

I got up early and took the short ride to Glacier. It was another great day for a ride. I was dressed for the chill of the mountains. The road is 50 miles long and starts out along the shore of Lake McDonald and then climbs to high country along "The Garden Wall". This road is narrow with many sharp turns, and no guardrails. The road crosses the Continental Divide at 6,680 feet. Along the way I would see Bighorn sheep along the cliffs, and the glaciers that carved the Waterton Valley below. The glaciers also carved the Garden wall, which is a jagged, sharp edged ridge. This ride was worth the 500 mile detour. You could easily spend a week here. The mountain and valley views, the wildlife, and the pure exhilaration of the motorcycling, added up to an interesting, exciting, and unforgettable experience.

Gary P. Stockbridge

GLACIER NATIONAL PARK

GOING TO THE SUN ROAD

I would leave the park and pick up route 89 south. As far as the relaxing aspect of motorcycling goes, this is it! I have never ridden better roads than in Montana. I could now see why they call it *"BIG SKY COUNTRY"*. The song Home, Home on the Range kept playing in my head. You could really lose yourself out here, just daydreaming, and the next thing you know you've ridden another hundred miles. I was traveling at 80 mph or more all day. I would stay in Great Falls, Montana that night. The following day I would continue on until Livingston Montana. The gateway to Yellowstone and Wyoming.

Livingston is a great little town. With it's old restored buildings, it had an undeniable charm. But still a little rough around the edges. Not "yuppy-ized". I had a few beers in a saloon that night, and some good conversation with a quite attractive local girl about 25 years old. I would soon get the feeling from a man in the bar that I better cool it. I did. After all "I was just passin' through".

I ended up camping that night in Gardiner. Which is the entrance into the north side of Yellowstone. It wasn't a campground as much as an R.V. park. It was o.k., but a lot of vehicles, and generators, and people. I would be on the road into Yellowstone at the crack of dawn. I had an idea about what I would be seeing, but when you're there it's another story, and I couldn't wait. By this time in my trip I was getting it all down to a science. I could break down my tent, pack up and get moving in less than an hour. I didn't always have the luxury of a shower but I managed to keep myself reasonably clean.

Yellowstone was America's first national park. Established in 1872. Teddy Roosevelt was a crusader for the national parks and he dedicated this one in person. "For the benefit and enjoyment of the people". The railroad brought the first visitors. There was a Railroad station in Livingston. It has since been restored, but it is now a museum.

There was a major fire in Yellowstone in 1989 in which 900,000 acres burned. There was evidence of this throughout the park. At first glance you might think, what an awful disaster. I would soon learn that this is a very natural and necessary force in nature. Already you could see the regeneration of the forest. The wildflowers seemed especially brilliant set against the black forest floor. The tree saplings were very small, but they were a sign of regrowth.

This was turning out to be a very hot, and very dry summer. The moisture content was 9 percent in 1989 and was 10 percent now. The fire danger was very high and there were restrictions on campfires.

There is no other place on earth that offers what Yellowstone does. The geologic features in addition to the wildlife, mountains, and virgin forests. This is truly a magical place and I don't mean "disney magic". I always try to get going at dawn for the solitude and the wildlife. Everything changes later on with all the tourists and vehicles.

The first of the natural wonders I saw, was the Mammoth Hot Springs. I had never seen anything like this before, and I found it fascinating. There was a smell of sulfur in the air at a lot of these features throughout the park. The hot water from below, forces it's way up through limestone terraces, where the air, water, and steam, escape from the ground. In some places slowly, and some places, explosively.

I ended up getting a campsite at Madison Junction, in the center of the park. I set up my stuff and went off to explore. There is one thing after another to see, and I saw a lot. I saw the Mud Pots, the Fountain Basin, and of course Old Faithful, where I also had a few beers. On the way back from Old Faithful the traffic started to slow down, so I veered a little to the left to see what was up. There was a herd of bison in the grass field up ahead. They were walking towards the road. Then the traffic stopped and the bison began walking down the road towards me. At this point my heart started to pound a little bit. These animals weigh between 1100 and 2000 pounds and they were heading my way! They can be aggressive if they feel threatened. There was one particular bull that walked so close to me I could of touched his nose. He looked right at me and I looked right at him. It was both scary and exciting at the same time. This place is wild!

The sun was setting as I headed back to camp. There was very little light left, when I came across a herd of Roosevelt Elk among the trees. I also saw several coyote. When I arrived back at my camp there had been a bear sighting and a ranger was warning everyone and instructing them on what "not" to do. I would be heading out of the park in the morning, and again it seemed too soon.

There are prairie dogs everywhere around here. They are really comical. They stick together and nervously pop up there heads and warn each other of danger with their calls. They were all around as I was packing up to leave. Next stop, The Grand Tetons.

The Grand Teton National Park sits directly below Yellowstone, in Wyoming, and route 89 takes you right into it. The first thing of note after passing through The John D. Rockefeller National Forest was the beautiful Jackson Lake, and route 89 was running right along it's shore.

The Rocky mountains were now behind me and Jackson Lake was to my right. Then the Tetons. For sheer drama these mountains are unmatched. I think the thing that adds to this, is the fact that there are no foothills in front of them. Teewinot mountain is the first peak you see heading south. Then Mount Owen. Then Teton Glacier and then Grand Teton at 13,770 feet above sea level. There are five peaks in all. They are jagged and abrupt, and have more than a dozen mountain glaciers. The forest at the base and the lake all added to an incredibly beautiful view.

It was along this road that the traffic came to a stop. I took advantage of this by getting off my bike to stretch my legs and take a few pictures. Others were doing the same and one guy noticed my Mass. plate and struck up a conversation. His name was Mike and he was from Mass. as well. He had just gotten out of the Army, and was driving home across the country with a friend that also just got out. We were both on our way to Jackson Hole for the night and we decided to get together for a few beers.

Jackson Hole is a very wealthy resort town, most of it's money is made during the ski season. There was a lodge at the base of the mountain and that's where these guys were staying. It was too rich for my blood. The resort also had this motel style building that you could stay as well. If you wanted to share a room it would be even cheaper. That's what I did.

I took a nap for a few hours, and met those guys at the lodge bar, at about nine. The band was just getting started and the place was filling up. There were a lot of women and I tried for a little while to meet someone. I wasn't having any luck, so I decided to just concentrate on inebriate. I drank a little too much that night. But it was a good time.

I would be heading north again the following morning, and back through Yellowstone. These guys were doing the same and we decided to stick together for a while. This time through I saw something I had missed the first time. The Grand Canyon of Yellowstone and The Lower Falls. This 308 foot waterfall was the best I have seen. The walls in this canyon are yellow, hence the name.

"GRAND CANYON OF YELLOWSTONE"

Mike mentioned "Bear tooth road," and said it was supposed to be good. It sounded good to me. We decided to take it and head towards Red Lodge, Montana.

The Bear tooth Highway was completed in 1936. It is one of the highest and most rugged areas in the lower 48. There are over twenty peaks reaching over 12,000 feet. There are black bears, grizzlies, mountain goats, moose, and a lot of smaller animals as well. This road travels through three national forests and connects Livingston Montana, and Red Lodge. It's almost 70 miles long and takes over three hours to travel. It was cold up there.

We stayed in the small, old mining town, of Red Lodge that night. We had a spaghetti dinner in town and we decided we were going to go see George H.W. Bush in Billings, Montana the next day.

It was about this time I was starting to have an electrical problem with my bike. It would just shut off unexpectedly. The guys agreed to help me out the next day, and help me get my bike to a shop.

I found a Kawasaki shop and made an appointment to have it fixed. The electrical problem, new tires, and an oil change.

The following morning we drove up to Billings, found a motel with a pool, hung out for a while, and then they followed me to the shop. It was a thirty mile ride. This was very appreciated. I left the bike and then we went to see George.

It was Friday, July 20, 1990 and George Bush was giving an anti-drug speech at Daylis stadium. When he arrived he waved in my direction. I was surprised at the lack of security. It was fun and different, I had never seen a president before.

The following morning these guys would be dropping me off and then they were going to Chicago.

I decided I was going to go to South Dakota. Once again, great people out here on the road.

We all slept late that day. We got going around 11:00. They dropped me off at the shop and they were on their way. My bike was ready to go. It turns out there was a frayed wire rubbing on the frame. I paid my bill and I was on my way.

I thought this was going to be one of those easy days that you don't have to think too much. Just get on the highway and drive. I was planning on staying on Route 90 all day, but, there was a split, and I mistakenly ended up on Route 94, and heading north. Route 90 started heading southeast at the split, but I missed it. I drove about 150 miles when I saw a sign that read "125 miles to North Dakota". The only problem was, I wasn't going to North Dakota. So I stopped to read my maps. My mistake had basically cost me about 300 miles.

Chapter Seven

The Badlands

Since I didn't know the area I chose the shortest route to make up for my mistake, and to get back on track. If you are looking at your map it is the upper right hand corner of Wyoming, coming from Montana that my trouble started. I was trying to take route 212 to route 112 when I ran out of pavement on the border of the two states. I could see where the pavement picked up again in about a quarter mile. It was inexplicable to me why they wouldn't just finish it up.

The road ahead was very muddy, So, I stopped again to read my maps, hoping that I missed something the first time I looked. This was not turning out to be a good day. I had to decide to turn around again, and go another 100 miles out of my way.....or....try and make it. I decided to try and make it. This stuff didn't look like the mud back home, and I would soon find out why.

I rolled off the pavement at about 5 m.p.h. and immediately began to slip around. It felt like I was riding in pudding. My first strategy was to just keep it moving and stay out of the ruts if possible. Then the front wheel slipped into the rut, and pointed me sideways a little, so I gave it more gas and tried to correct it. Game time. I was off the road and over.

I tried and tried to pull it out. Half the bike was off the edge of the road and the nose was down about a foot or so. There was no way. My feet were slipping around too much and I had no leverage.

I knew there was nothing for fifty miles the way I came in. So, my only choice was to walk forward, and there was nothing in sight in that direction either. I was covered in mud. I walked...and walked....and walked... for more than a mile when I came to a restaurant. Thank God.

I walked in, and there were three guys at the breakfast counter. They turned around and looked. They laughed at me, and then asked, " Did you dump?" "Yeah, I fell about a mile back, " " can you guys give me a hand?" Before they had a chance to reply, I offered them money. They agreed to help me out and then they told me about Bentonite.

It's basically clay, and it is extremely slippery. They told me they mine the stuff out here. It's used for all sorts of things. Like soap, toothpaste, cements, ceramics, and a lot of other things. That's what I was riding on....or in.

Well, they had their laugh, and I had to admit I looked pretty funny. Then I climbed into the back of a pickup and we drove back there. The four of us got it out of there pretty easily, and before they helped pull me out, I had them take my picture. We got the bike back on the road and pointing in the right direction. They offered to push me until I got to pavement. That was generous, because they would of gotten muddy. I said I would ride it. "Are you sure?" they asked. "yeah, I'll make it". I gave them $20.00 and I said "thank you", and got on my bike and started riding. I was all over the place, but I made it. They must of been laughing their asses off watching me ride out.

I was now in Wyoming and I stopped for breakfast about an hour down the road. I ate everything. Pancakes, toast, eggs, coffee, and drank about a half gallon of milk. I noticed a hose outside, so I asked the owner (who was also the cook) if I could use it. Since he hadn't seen my bike, he said "yeah sure, go ahead". There was clay everywhere. I must of left 10 pounds there on the ground. I tried to wash it away, but I was not completely successful. Right as I was done, he came out. He wasn't too happy with me. I said I was sorry, and told him about my mishap. He didn't seem moved.

I found a motel nearby and checked in. There were some people at the motel on bicycles. I asked them how far they had ridden, and they said, New York. I couldn't imagine how hard that would be. Especially in this heat, on a bicycle. Wow! I had an engine and I thought what I was doing was difficult!

So, the sun was up and I was once again packing to go, and it was a good day for a ride. I was still in Wyoming, and I would be in South Dakota very soon. The only problem was, I felt like I was in a fight the night before, and my bike now had a wobble in it. The fairing was bent about two inches to one side from my little accident.

I looked at my map, and began to head south towards the Badlands, when I came upon The Devils Tower. This thing is wild! I knew I had seen it before but I didn't know where, I would later remember it was from the movie "Close Encounters Of The Third Kind". Remember the scene when he's making this massive clay sculpture? This is what he was making. This is the Black Hills region of Wyoming.

DEVILS TOWER

Devils Tower rises 1,267 feet above the Belle Fourche River. It's almost shaped like an upside down cone, with one half cut off. The sides have deep gorges, closely spaced all the way around. This place is a sight that you will never forget. The best part was, I wasn't expecting it, I didn't know about it, and it caught me by complete surprise.

There is an old Indian legend about the tower. It says that three young indian women were gathering flowers, when they were approached by bears. They climbed on the large rock to escape. The bears could easily climb the rock, so the gods thrust the stone up out of the ground. The bears clung to the side, and clawed deep gashes in the rock, until they fell and died. The maidens then made rope from the flowers that they had picked, and safely lowered themselves to the ground.

I wonder what ever happened to those maidens. I could use a maiden now, I remember thinking. The road was getting to me.

Next stop, Mount Rushmore. It turned out that there was a B.M.W. motorcycle rally there. I pulled in on my rice-rocket and surveyed the scene. A mass of bikers, and The Mount Rushmore Monument up above. This, being a man made attraction, was impressive nonetheless. It took 400 men, 13 years, to sculpt the 60-foot busts of Washington, Jefferson, Roosevelt, and Lincoln out of the granite. It was built by Gutzon Borgium and was completed in 1941.

I arrived at Badlands National Park at dusk, which was perfect. The Black Hills rose up out of the surrounding prairie. Entering the park, the landscape looked so foreign to anything I had ever seen before, and seemed other-worldly. The colors, and harshness of the terrain, and the solitude, all added up to a spooky and foreboding landscape. The only living thing I saw was a coyote. This place is loaded with prehistoric history, and there are displays set up to check out. The colors and the shadows were changing constantly, and the range of colors was remarkable. There were rusty reds, sandy yellows, and light browns. The surface of the rock was course, sharp, and angular. I couldn't imagine what it must of been like for the Sioux people to live out here. There have been humans here for over 11,000 years. The Sioux (also called Lakota), arrived in the mid eighteenth century. They hunted bison, and would only be here 100 years. They fought to keep their land, but in the end they would be pushed on to reservations after the

Wounded Knee Massacre in 1890. 300 Sioux and 25 American soldiers were killed in this battle.

In the name of progress, wheat fields would replace the prairies, and horses would replace the bison. The bison were hunted to near extinction by our ancestors. The Sioux would be followed by trappers, soldiers, miners, cattle farmers, and homesteaders.

The Badlands National Monument was established in 1939 by Franklin D. Roosevelt. 130,000 acres of Ogala Sioux tribal land was added in the sixties. This land was used since World War Two as a U.S. Air Force bombing range. The Ogala Sioux signed an "agreement" in 1976. The park now consists of 244,000 acres. The sharply eroded buttes and spires of the park are surrounded by the largest prairie in America. There are once again bison roaming the land.

I had a long way to go until I was ... home. I had ridden about 9,500 miles and I was out in the middle of the country and heading straight east. It was sinking in, the trip was winding down, but I saw so much in such a short time that I could use some time to process it all.

Many people I had met along the way, said they dreamed of doing what I was doing. The demands and responsibilities of life always get in the way. There is also the time and the money aspect. You need both. There is always a trade off. I was doing this, but other's choose marriage, and children, and what they get is awesome. I was thirty years old, single, and no children. I had no regrets about the choices I made. I really never envisioned the married bliss thing for me. I never felt that I was cut out for it. But, my mother used to say I just haven't met the right one. There were a few that I thought were right, but unfortunately those ladies didn't feel the same about me.

Friends asked me jokingly. Did you find yourself? The fact is the road gives you a lot of time to think. Let's face it, my professional life and personal life at this time were not especially satisfying to me. I had a lot of friends and I was having a lot of fun. Going out, partying, hanging out at the local bar, drinking, smoking, getting high. But after the high wears off. What was I doing? Would I change when I got back? I didn't know. But, I did realize how big this country is, and beautiful, and diverse. People were great to me. Time would tell.

Chapter Eight

Iowa and Illinois

From South Dakota, I would be going to Sioux City, Iowa. I would pick up Route 20 there. Route 20 also runs from one side of the country to the other. It's the more northerly route, and I would be taking this the rest of the way home. Almost right to my door in Lexington, Mass.

Iowa sits between the Missouri and Mississippi river. There are 97, 000 farms in Iowa (at this writing), and those farms are the number one grower of corn in the nation.

Corn is all that I would be seeing for a long, long, lonnnnggg, time. Route 20 looks like a straight route on the map, but, it's left , right, left, right, for over 200 miles in Iowa. The amount of corn out here baffles the mind, and I enjoyed riding through here,...for the first 100 miles or so.

Maybe I was just a little weary. Let me correct that, very weary. I had called home and received some very bad news, and my attitude had changed. I will say more on this later.

There are things to see and do. You have two great rivers, and a riverboat casino in Sioux City. There is a lot of history as well. Lewis and Clark began their expedition from the Missouri heading west from here, and there are local museums and a downtown brewery.

If you are interested in fake history. There's the Cardiff Giant, a 7' foot tall skeleton, "unearthed" in New York in 1868. Experts thought they were bones of a prehistoric man. The skeleton was used by P.T. Barnum for the next 35 years. It was finally revealed that it had been carved from Gypsom. There is a replica in Fort museum in Fort Dodge.

If you saw the movie "Field of Dreams", you can visit the ballpark, and the surrounding area, where parts of the movie were filmed, in Dyerville, Iowa. I didn't do any of the things I just mentioned. I was strictly into heading east. I have done some research of things I missed, and will mention a few more of the attractions nearby.

Galena, Illinois is well worth checking out. It was a bustling town of 15,000 in the Civil War. The gold rush and economic hardship left the town virtually deserted. Ioo years would pass before they started to bring it back. Restored with historic accuracy, down to the hand carved signs, and back-in-time feel, this is a great place to stop and walk around.

Ulysses S. Grant was from Galena and you can visit the modest, restored home and museum, which I did in 2008. The town has plenty of choices for food and lodging. From Rockford to Chicago, Route 20 is a slow, winding road, through small towns, and past farms and fruit stands. The Illinois Railway Museum is in Union, Illinois. If you like trains, this is a great place to spend a couple of hours. I saw the Chicago skyline but I didn't go there. I know there is a lot to do, but I was thinking of home, and about money, I had about $500.00 left. I jumped on 90 and bypassed the city.

Chapter Nine

Rear View Mirror

What makes one person feel that motorcycling is the best possible thing you could do. Then the next person just can't understand why you would want to. People never seem to be lukewarm with their opinions on motorcycles, or their riders.

To some, all motorcyclists are biker-scum. These people seem to go out of their way, to get in yours. I actually had someone throw a door open in front of me because I was splitting the lane in a traffic jam. Yes, I was wrong, but to try and cause me to crash. That's sick. I have been cut off more times than I could count. People just don't seem to give an inch.

Then you have most other riders, They will wave, help you out if you need it, and go out of their way to talk to you. Most BMW riders I have seen on the road are snobs. But then again, those are just the ones on the fancy, expensive bikes. The people that ride the older, air-head models, are as down to earth as you could get. The Harley riders I don't understand. I must be clear here, I don't mean my brothers. They ride Harleys, but do not fit the stereotype. But for most, I think it's all about the look. They do not wave unless you ride a Harley.

When I started riding, the amount of abuse I took, just because I rode a japanese bike was ridiculous. But I always argued my point. After all, if freedom is the thing, then why do I have to ride, what you think I should ride, or wear the Harley uniform. Their argument would always fall apart when you start asking about all the other consumer goods they buy. Whether it's clothes, stereo, cars, camera, t.v, and a hundred other things. I have always driven Chevrolets, and I don't like Japanese cars, but I don't ridicule those that do. That would be idiotic.

I would love to live in an America, that offered all these things, made in the U.S.A.. But unfortunately that's not the case.

The thing that kills me the most, is the people that wear all the gear, and have all the tattoo's, and don't even ride. Then they have the nerve to put down your bike. To me the best thing about riding is the freedom and independence. These guys all dress the same, and a lot of them share the same opinions on rice burners.

My first high speed experience came on the back of my brother Bobby's motorcycle. I was about 14 or 15. My brother Bobby was about 25. He was cool, and was always good to me. He had a Kawasaki kz1000. He asked me if I wanted to take a ride with him. I said "yeah". He was going to pick up some pipes for it, and we had to go on the highway. Getting there was fine, he rode normal, but quickly. So, we're getting ready to start heading home and I put my helmet on, but not especially tight. There was no sissy bar, and I had his pipes under each arm. So, I basically had to lean forward to stay on. Then he accelerated, hard, and I actually considered dropping the pipes so that I could hold on. In the 30 seconds or so that it took him to get over 100 miles an hour, I was leaning so far forward, that my head was under his arm, and my helmet had come off and was choking me. That was an absolutely scary and exciting experience.

My brother Dickie was a wild one too. His nickname was Do-wrong. What an instigator. He loved to tease us kids. I used to have to protect my plate if he was nearby. I'm pretty sure he was the one who stuck me with a couple of nicknames that I wasn't particularly fond of. He once rode his motorcycle right into a curb in front of the supermarket, and was launched head first through a plate glass window. I think that was a triumph chopper. He had a lot of stitches in his head. But his face was O.K. and he was (is) very handsome.

My first riding was on a mini-bike, and then a dirt bike. My brother Bobby had a place in Wilmington, Mass., surrounded by woods and trails. He would let me go up to his house while he wasn't there, and use his stereo, and his motorcycle. This is when I was 17. He had two German Shepherds. There was Jessie, a huge, white dog, with a massive head and neck. He was very strong, and he was obsessed with retrieving things. Logs mostly, and sometimes rocks. He was very friendly, and had a great personality. This dog would open the door to the cottage and then close it after himself. The other dog was Nico. She had some emotional problems. But, she had a good soul. He had this huge, industrial size, bug zapper up there. Giant Bugs Fried Dead.

I hate to say it but my first ride on a full size motorcycle was my brother's Kawasaki. I didn't have permission. I didn't go far, I just practiced figure eights and slow maneuvers in a parking lot. I knew I wanted one.

The next few years in my house were crazy. There was trouble between my parents. Me and my younger sister Nancy, just couldn't get along. The youngest in the family, Scott, was caught in the middle of it all, and he was only 10. Between the ages of 6 and 10 for him, it was chaos in that house.

My brother David and I were close when I was kid. My early teen years he was good to me as well. I felt alone in that house, and he would take me out. He encouraged my drawing, and painting, and he took me to D.C. on a train one time. I realized then, that I liked travel. I liked just soaking it in, watching the people and learning about the country and history. Things that I didn't have much interest in, in the confines of school.

I did a lot of things that I shouldn't of done. I drank too much. I used drugs, and I did terrible in school. I totally failed grades 9 and 10 and received Zero credits and they still put me into 11th. I did work harder the next two years, and I went to a vocational school in the afternoon for graphic arts. I had to go to school from eight-thirty in the morning until five -forty -five. Just so I could have a *chance* to graduate. Which I did.

But on the weekends I would go nuts. I'm surprised I made it through. I know about eight people that ended up dead from the group that hung around Stoneham Square. At this time in my life I really didn't care too much about living or dying. I drove my cars recklessly and I used drugs heavily. My father was aware of this. He asked me if he could take out a life insurance policy on me. I agreed. What would I care. I would be dead.

My sister Susan was (is) a born-again Christian, and she had moved out and married by this time. But, she was always just a phone call away, to come and take my little sister Nancy, to settle her down. My poor mother. Things were so unhappy in that house. My mother was always crying, and she would stay in her room a lot. Long stretches of silence between my parents was normal. This affected all of us, and things between Nancy and I were so bad, that my father told us not to speak with each other. We didn't, for four years.

My father was cheating on my mother for years and we all knew it. There were phone calls at night, and hang-ups. I caught on to the routine and would try and pick up the phone upstairs. One time my father answered (while I was already on the line), and his girlfriend said, "someone is on the phone", and they hung up. Then I came downstairs and walked right by my father. He didn't say a word. My brother, actually caught my father with the other woman. Over the years, there was more than one woman. He would deny it, and tell my mother she was imagining it. This took a major toll on the home, especially for us last three kids. I think all this turmoil affected the relationship of my mother, and my sister Nancy. My mother was having a terrible time. Things were so unhappy in that house, that I told my father, that *he* should leave. He told me, that my mother would kill herself. I was around 12.

The relationship between my father and I, was not good. I received a lot of physical punishment. But, I was not abused. I wanted, so much sometimes, to just talk to my father. He was not available to me, and never seemed interested in me, at all. My siblings and my mother have told me how much my father loved me, when I was very young, and I believe them. But, when I was in need of my father, he was not only not there for me, he would put me down. I did not see this in his relationships to my brother's. One of my brother's was very close to my father, and my mother and that increased my pain. But, I always felt kind of like Hertz, I try harder.

My sister Susan or "Miss Suzie" as she is known in the church, was "born again" in the late seventies. She then brought her second husband, Jimmy and eventually most of my family. This was a "Holy Roller" type religion, complete with demons being cast out and healings. I went one time when I was about fifteen, to listen to "brother Joe", and witnessed speaking in tongues, and the violent contortions of a man posessed. It scared the hell out of me and I never went back.

This was a confusing time for me, because I could no longer relate on any level with my brother David, my two sisters, or to a lesser extent my brother

Bobby. He was never as over-the-top as the others. From some, I felt that everything I did was judged. To maintain a relationship, you would have to go along with all that they said, listen to their constant citing of scripture, and be very careful of what you say. If there was any music you were excited about, or movie you saw, or anything considered "worldly", you just had to keep it to yourself. My girlfriend didn't like being around them because of their views of us, as "sinners". One time we were accused of fornicating in my sister's house. What we were doing was playing scrabble. It must of been the messy hair. Give me a break! My brother Dickie was never into any of this. My little brother Scott, was going through some very tough times too. He's six years younger than me. We got along fine. We did a lot of the wrong things together.

The church grew to about 200 people and they were all convinced the Lord was coming back "soon". I remember 1984 being mentioned. These seemed to be very good times for them. These were good times for me as well. Outside the family. My good times were mainly chemical or alcohol related before I started riding, once I bought my first motorcycle I had a great outlet, and escape from all the drama and confusion.

The family situation started to fracture when people started to leave the church. My brother Bobby pulled his family out. David pulled his out. The church attendance was dropping way off. Susan would attribute this to "the devil". There were and are deep wounds that haven't healed, as a result of these divisions. The Bible says to forgive, but from my perspective, I don't see forgiveness. I don't know what the reasons are, but my family was closer before "religion". This doesn't mean that I have lost faith. I still believe in God, and that Jesus died for our sins, and rose again. I hope for mercy.

My first car was a 14 year old, 1963 Chevrolet Impala wagon. It had a 327 four barrel with dual exhaust, and 300 horsepower. People would laugh when I wanted to race with this wagon. I surprised a lot of people.

My next car was a 1965 Oldsmobile Dynamic 88, with a 425. It was a beater, the hood was tied down with a piece of rope and one hinge was broken off. I paid $100.00. Regardless, I took that car up on the highway and did 100 miles and hour on route 93, with the hood flapping until the rope broke, and the hood swung towards the drivers side and scraped on the ground, sparks flying. I loved it. My father ended up junking that car on me when I drove it home one time with an electrical fire.

I hung around with my cousin Richie (a.k.a. Abbott) a lot at this time. He loved the Crown Royal. This kid was a character. He was driving his fathers Chrysler Imperial one night in particular. This car had been in an accident previously, and was pretty much totaled, or at least I thought so. Well, anyway I was waiting for him one night, in a dirt parking lot down at the boy's club in Woburn, near Central Square, there was no-one else around when he pulled in. I had him in T-Bone position. I revved my engine until it screamed, and I was laughing my ass off. He realized what I was thinking, and with great emphasis, waved no. I put it in drive, and nailed the gas, slammed into his right rear quarter, doing about 30, and pushed his tail end about 15 feet. Then my car stalled and he maneuvered his car to ram me in reverse, he took his time, he allowed himself about 30 yards to get up speed. I was franticly trying to get my car started. Then, looking out the back window of his car as he looked right at me, hit the gas, built up good speed, and nailed me. That was it. I needed a new radiator, and hood. "Too funny", we used to say, back in the seventies.

Looking back, I'm glad I wasn't riding a bike at this time. I never thought I would live to thirty as it was.

My brother Bobby had 1952 Harley Panhead at around this same time, within a couple of years or so. What a machine, he had just had it done over. It was a metallic light brown and was just the right balance of chrome and paint. It wasn't all loaded up with extras. I wouldn't of dared take this one for a ride. It was a beauty.

Apparently this bike caught the eye of a local motorcycle gang. The Devils Disciples. The leader of the gang went up to my brother's little house in Wilmington and stole it. There was a trick to turning the lights on and the thief was pursued at high speed on the highway with no lights on, when he crashed and died. I remember my mother crying when it was on the news.

They held my brother responsible, and he was in serious danger. He had to stay at a safe house for awhile. The biker's robbed his house. Fortunately my brother had a lot of friends, and he found the right person to broker peace, through a kangaroo court of sorts, and he even got most of his stuff back. But the bike was gone. What a waste.

My brother David started his own "bike gang". The Lost Cause. They had their dungaree coats, with cutoff arms, with their colors proudly displayed on the back. A motorcycle gang didn't appreciate this and pulled their jackets. The only thing was, these were teenagers and they were riding bicycles.

The first person I ever heard about, that got seriously messed up riding a motorcycle, was a friend of my brother's. I saw him right before it happened. I was painting my parent's house with my brother (pivothead painters) when he stopped by. His name is Steve Bornstein. I was told he had a fight with his girlfriend, and was angry. He was traveling at about 80 miles an hour on main street, when an old lady pulled out in front of him. He was launched about 40 yards, and ended up paralyzed from the neck down. He has been in the hospital for the last thirty years.

I was just a rookie in the printing business, and still bikeless, in 1979, when I met a girl, or she met me. Norwegian wood. I fell in love, and settled down, and started doing all the couple things, and hanging around with all the couples. I was getting a little bit domesticated. We talked every day if we didn't see each other. We talked about marriage, and children, and how cute they would be. I still saw my friends but not nearly as frequently. It was really a match made in heaven for the next three years, and I was totally in love with this girl. She was beautiful and kind, and she loved me.

Then things changed. We would drink and argue, and argue and drink, and argue some more. Then I got depressed, but I didn't know what it was. I just knew I felt like I wanted to die. I was self medicating a lot at this time. Then she cheated on me, and I found out through a friend. I didn't trust her anymore. It was over.

I did two things at this point. I bought a motorcycle and joined the Elks. What a combination. I knew everyone at the Elks, and all my friends were joining. My cousin Larry was a member. They had a pool table and pinball, Big screen t.v, and we would blast the M.T.V.. We were the younger generation and we sure livened that place up. Maybe a little too much. There were several members that were cops. That must of been a test for them, considering some of the things that were going on. It was the eighties and "everybody" was doing it. The real thing.

The bike was a 1978 Kawasaki kz 650. I think I paid $900.00 for it. Along with the bike, the seller gave me some good advice. He told me to always look for a way out, and always expect people to do the stupidest thing. That advice saved me more than once.

The speed of that bike was absolutely scary. If you turned the throttle too fast, you had to hang on for dear life. I was not yet a skilled, smart, or mature rider. These things came into play one night on Massachusetts Avenue in Cambridge. I pulled up to a stop light next to another Kawasaki. He looked at me, and I looked at him, and we both revved our engines.

It was on, the light turned green and we both gunned it. His front wheel came off the ground, but he never let off the gas. In less than 6 seconds we were doing 70 m.p.h. and he was riding a wheelie. He was still a little bit in front of me, on one wheel! Then he started to tilt to the left, and the nose came down just in time to smash head-on into a curb on the median strip. It was like slow motion, I was right beside him. His bike crumpled like aluminum foil, and he was sent sliding down the street on his ass. Luckily there was no oncoming traffic, but he slid at least thirty yards, feet first into a curbstone. He was asking how the bike was even though there was a bone protruding through the top of his sneaker. The bike was scrap metal and he was lucky. It wasn't even his bike.

Chapter Ten

Indiana and Ohio

Back to 1990, and heading past Chicago and into Indiana. I once again got off of route 90 and back on 20. I was very weary, but I couldn't stand the freeway for long stretches. This part of Indiana, on route 20, is not particularly interesting and the road is basic city driving. The one thing that stands out in my mind is the smell of Gary, Indiana. It was very hot when I passed through, and the haze of industry hung in the air, and the fumes would choke you. This is one of the most heavily industrialized parts of the country, and massive petrochemical plants are surrounded by impoverished communities. It got so bad in the sixties in this area, with stripped out cars, decay and crime, that the National Guard had to police the streets.

Twenty- five miles east of Chicago, you come upon the Indiana Dunes National Seashore, on the shore of Lake Michigan. There are sand dunes, and fresh water beaches. There are trees, grassland and hiking trails. A good place to stop. I kept going.

East of South Bend, the road becomes a lot more agreeable. Middlebury and Shipshewana are in the heartland of Indiana's agricultural heartland. This is also Amish country.

If you are an antique car enthusiast, the Auburn-Cord-Dusenberg Museum is in Auburn. This is 20 miles south of route 20. Considered by most, to be the most beautiful, innovative, and the highest quality machines ever produced in the United States. The Auburns and Cords were produced in Auburn during the 20's and 30's. The "Dusies" were made in Indianapolis. There are 150 cars on display, including Rolls-Royce, Packards and Cadillacs, in a beautiful art-deco showroom. I do wish I knew about this when I was there. I definitely would love to see those cars.

Earlier in the trip I crossed Ohio on route 50 heading west. Now I was in northern Ohio on route 20, and heading east, and like before the roads are good and the barns with the faded "Chew Mail Pouch Tobacco" painted on their sides, are all over the state. It was this part of the country that was "The Anvil Of America". From the late 1800's to the 1950's the bulk of the country's iron, steel, and petroleum products were made here. This is the Lake Erie shore.

The northeast part of Ohio will take you passed rolling farmland, and along the Lake Erie shore, to the small town of Ashtabula. This is a large boating port for pleasure boats.

Pennsylvania on route 20 is only fifty miles or so. Then New York. I was only two states away from my home state of Massachusetts. The trip was winding down and I was getting close to home.

When I was in South Dakota I had called home, and I was told about a sudden death in the family. My cousin Kenny was six years older than me and he grew up on the next street to mine. When I was just a kid, I thought he was so cool. He would play some of his favorite music for me, and cheerfully demonstrate his chops on the piano. He was always a little rough around the edges and that was part of what I liked. I think I was around ten when he showed me his brass knuckles. During his teen years, like many other kids in the late sixties and early seventies, he started using drugs. He died from heroin use in July 1990.

I felt awful being so far away (South Dakota) when I found out. There was no way I could make it home. My mind was in a fog, and I missed my family.

Cassie and Raisa were about six weeks old by now, and I was anxious to see them. Cassie is my Goddaughter. I have a lot of other nieces and nephews. I think in 1990 I had about 19 or so. My sister Susan had an adopted daughter named Alayne, and would later adopt a little boy named J.J., and my cousin Kenny's daughter, Leah. My brother Bobby had four boys, Joshua, Caleb, Matthew, and Robert. My brother Dickie had three girls, Kate (my Godchild), Jesse, and Ashley. My brother David had four girls, Cortney, Cristen, Shannon, and Raisa. My sister Nancy had three children at this time, Jalyn, Zachary, Noelle, and Gabrielle would come later. My brother Scott had Cassie. He would later have Mike and Sarah. Of course none of these children would have happened without their spouses. James, Maeva, Debra, Ellen, Buddy, and Michele, respectively.

I had called my mother once from California. She's a great lady. Very warm and kind and thoughtful. She hated motorcycles and all five of her sons rode them. She didn't like it when I used to say that I was going to "hit the road".

Chapter Eleven

New York State

Route 20 runs almost parallel to I-90, and it's a good road, and a much better choice than the madness of the Interstate. It will take you by the Finger Lakes (a great trip in it's own right), then through the Hudson Valley, near Albany, and eventually you begin the gradual incline of The Taconic Mountains before coming to the Berkshire foothills, close to the Massachusetts border.

Westfield and Chautaqua county is the home to some of the states finest wineries and vineyards. Westfield also has the distinction of having the nickname "Grape Juice Capital of The World". The Concord grape was introduced here in 1859. In 1897 Dr. Charles Welch and his father founded Welch Foods.

Of course there is Niagara Falls to see, if you want to detour. I had never been there at the time, and at this point in my trip I was bone tired and burnt out. I wasn't soaking in all that was around me like I was in the beginning. I was kind of on auto-pilot. Not to say this isn't a great place to see, it is. The waterfall is awesome, but the surrounding area, is a bit too commercial.

The road will take you by farmlands and pastures, and through rolling hills, and into quaint little towns as it winds it's way east.

The weather was still cooperating completely. Of course I have had to deal with heat, and cold, and wind, and fog, but very little rain. Weather is the X-factor when it comes to riding a motorcycle. You can make all the plans you want, but if the weather is bad enough you're not going anywhere. My feeling on rain is, if I'm already on the road and traveling, and I have a destination, I will press on unless there is serious danger. I once took a trip to New Orleans that I was planning for a long time. It was raining on the day I left, and it rained every day (sometime torrential) for the entire two week vacation. With the exception of one day. That day, was the 24 hours I spent in New Orleans. That trip, was a marathon, and a test. I got caught on the Blue Ridge Parkway with rain so heavy, and fog so thick, I just had to stop.

There was no cover whatsoever. I finally creeped my way down the mountain to find myself at the bottom, at a red light, with the water flowing like a river down the street, and around my feet. Probably 1" or 2" deep. I found a motel, and the weatherman said there was no end in sight. Rain complicates everything. Packing up in the morning, and breaking down at night, is a challenge to keep things dry. Once the chill gets into your bones, it's hard to get out. By the end of the day you are bowlegged, hunched over, and your hands are more like claws, and are practically useless. Getting change out of your pocket with cold, lobster claw hands, into wet pants, is a joke.

The roads around the Finger Lakes are good, but you will have to detour off of route 20 to enjoy the best of this area. Several years after this trip I went back there, and drove 1000 miles round trip, from my home, around the Finger Lakes and back. The roads are graceful and long, and lightly traveled. If you look on a map you will notice the unique pattern of the lakes. The Iroquois Indians believed this was the hand print of God. While there, I saw a pair of mature Bald Eagles in a tree. I spent some time in Watkins Glen when I was there. This is a car racing town with a couple of tracks. There is a great natural feature of Watkins Glen that has man made paths deep into this mini canyon, with many waterfalls. This is Watkins Glen State Park. It's right in the center of town. It was so cool, literally and figuratively.

Seneca Falls is worth checking out. This was the birthplace of the women's movement in 1848. The Erie Canal is worth checking out as well and you can take boat trips down the canal from here. The Erie Canal Museum is in Syracuse.

Cooperstown is along the way (20 mile detour), and if you love baseball it's a must-do. I didn't do it at this time, but I went back there several years ago, and I loved it. The Babe Ruth stuff was cool to see, but bittersweet being a Red Sox fan. I went there, the same year that Sosa and Mcguire were battling the entire season, and broke the home run record. They were both later tainted by steroids. There is a great little lake there as well. Plenty of choices for food and souvenirs. There is also a massive native American artifacts collection at the Fenimore House Museum.

UPDATE- SOX WIN WORD SERIES! TWICE! 2004 AND 2007!

I don't really remember where I stopped to sleep on many of the nights through this part of the trip. But, I can say that it was in a motel. My days sleeping on the ground were over. The routine was always the same. I would find a motel that didn't look like a total dive, then again, not too nice either. I would check in. By this time, I was using my credit card, almost all the cash was gone. Then I would unpack. My bike had two hard saddlebags on the back, and I hung a pair of soft saddlebags over the middle. In one of the hard bags I kept all the clothes, both dirty and clean, in a plastic bag. The other hard bag, I kept my rain gear, and leather jacket and sweatshirt, and other stuff I would put on and take off during the day. On the back seat I had my tent and sleeping bag, and full size helmet. In the left soft bag I kept all my maps and travel related books and pamphlets, all in Zip-Loc bags. In the right one I kept my camera related stuff, again in 1 gallon Zip-Loc bags.

Once in the motel room I would keep everything except the toiletries on the bed next to me. Just so I didn't have to look around too much in the morning.

Early on in the trip, I was up early and anxious to hit the road. Now, I was sleeping late and covering about 200 miles a day. I was still enjoying myself as much as I could, but I knew the best was behind me.

When I left Lexington, Massachusetts, I had rented out my room, because I wasn't sure when I would be back, and I wanted the bills to be paid. We agreed that when I came back, the sub-let would leave. He was using all my stuff and he had a good deal. I was thinking about this a little bit.

Reality was setting in. I was going back to unemployment (without the check) and no savings. The future was unclear, but I was confident that I would be back to work soon.

It was now very late July and I had driven over 11,000 miles. I had spent roughly $5,000 dollars between cash and credit. My budget when I started was 75 dollars a day. That obviously didn't work out. I had about 15 rolls of exposed film in my saddlebag and I was hopeful to have a lot of good pictures.

As far as romance on the road there really wasn't any. One night in Billings, Montana I spent the evening in a bar, in the company of a very attractive girl, and that was a lot of fun, but that was about it. She asked me if I would be in town the next night, and I said no. Maybe I should of stayed over. Romance on the road, or at home, has been elusive to me. I once spent the day riding with a girl I met on the road (she was riding a BMW), and we stayed at the same motel. She told me to call her, and we would go out for dinner. But, I was off by one room when I knocked on her door.

I saw her at breakfast and she asked me what happened. I told her that I knocked on her door, but there was no answer. Guess what? Wrong room! What an idiot. She was going to Halifax, Nova Scotia and I was going to Cape Breton, Nova Scotia. She invited me to go with her and meet her friends, I didn't. I had my mind set on Cape Breton and it was one of the best rides I have ever taken. I always wondered what might of been.

Then there was the night in New Orleans in 1987. I was by myself and having fun. But a little lonely. I started walking along beside the prettiest girl I saw, and asked her if she was going my way. She put her arm in mine and I had one of the best nights of my life. We danced and drank and danced some more. I felt like all eyes were on us. I was in rare form and she was gorgeous. As the clock got towards midnight, she told me she would like to spend the night with me, but she would have to charge me. I was shocked. I had no idea whatsoever. She was a prostitute! I considered it for a minute, but then I said no, with great disappointment. Then she suggested that I could just buy her things, if I was more comfortable with that. I still said no. Once I knew she was a prostitute the thought of being robbed entered my mind. We had spent about four hours together and I had no clue. We separated at that point with a tender kiss. My heart broken once more.

I ended up getting lost on my way back to the hotel and ended up in a bad section. I actually got directions from a guy I saw getting out of a dumpster. I gave him ten dollars and told him to have breakfast on me. He probably bought booze. New Orleans is a great city but I wouldn't go back alone.

Chapter Twelve
Home Stretch

Before noon, sometime around August first, I crossed over the Taconic mountains of New York, and into the Berkshires of Massachusetts. I had driven this route once or twice a year as long as I have been driving. The road has plenty of sweeping turns, some hard corners, and one Hairpin. The road is challenging at points, and very relaxing, and Sunday morning type of driving in others. This is no longer route 20. That is south of here. This road is known as the Mohawk Trail, it runs from the northwest corner of Massachusetts across the north of Massachusetts.

One of the first towns on route 2, before actually being on "The Mohawk Trail" is North Adams. This town, for as long as I can remember, has been enduring serious economic problems. But, due to the recent addition of The Museum of Contemporary Art, is now experiencing revitalization.

The Mohawk Trail, takes it's name from the path that the Mohawks used for raids on the Algonquian Indians. This was one of the nation's first scenic highways and was paved around 1914. The economically starved western part of the state, hoped for the help of tourists for survival. The best part of the road is east of the western summit. It hugs along the Cold River and is a real challenge, and a blast for motorcycling. This section will test your skills and quicken your pulse. If your lucky you'll find that place, where you just look where you want to go, and before you know it, it's behind you and your looking five seconds ahead and not even thinking, just riding. Concentrating on nothing but the turns and seeing almost nothing else. A great stretch of road.

Down into the valley you'll come upon the lazy Deerfield river. Then a touristy section of stores with wigwams and lots of kitschy trinkets. You won't learn anything here, but it's all in good fun, and I still like seeing it. I usually stop and get some homemade fudge and a cold drink.

If you want to take a small detour, checking out Shelburne Falls is worth it. The towns of Shelburne and Colrain are connected by a bridge. The bridge is no longer used, it's a trolley bridge that hasn't been used since the 1920's. Every fall local gardeners decorate the bridge with flowers. Hence the name "Bridge of Flowers".

Route 116 is a great alternative to route 2 if you happen to be traveling during foliage season (less traffic). It runs from Ashfield to Conroy. But, north to south instead of east to west. You'll pass several covered bridges and beautiful, pastoral, countryside.

Deerfield has a great historical story, as well as great architecture. English settlers waged a bloody war here against the Pocumtuck Indians. All over the country the story of the Indians is played out over and over, and always the same ending.

Once you cross the Connecticut River, the road gets wider and straighter and travels through roughly 30 miles of forest.

Concord has a lot to see, including Walden Pond, The Old North Bridge, and a lot of history from the Revolutionary War. The same can be said for Lexington. This town never shines brighter than Patriots day, with it's re-enactments and parade, and countless historical attractions. The Minuteman National Park is one of my favorite places in the area. This is only 10 minutes from my home and the surrounding landscape is being respectfully restored to the way it was in 1776. They are actually removing structures to leave open space.

As I approached route 128, I was only several miles from home. It was hot, oppressive, humid, and hazy. I decided to stop by my brother Scott's house before I even went home. I wanted to see Cassie. She was beautiful, and as healthy as could be. I was glad to be home. I would see Raisa later, and she was a beautiful, bouncing, happy baby, as well.

Then the short 2 mile road to my house. It was evening when I got there and there was no-one around except Ina the Airedale. She was happy to see me. I went upstairs to see if the guy I rented my room to was still there. He had left and he took some of my furniture with him.

I unpacked for the *LAST* time. I had driven 11,800 miles, give or take 50 or so. I had seen so much, in such a fast and compressed way, that I felt this sense of movement, and images, for about a week or so. Flashes of things that I saw for a split second, somewhere out on the road, would pop into my mind. I don't know what this was exactly, but it just seemed like my brain was still downloading all this stuff.

I went down the Elks to see my buddies and relax, and everyone was eager to hear about my travels. For some reason, some of them seemed to enjoy the negative stuff more. The bar looked exactly the same, and the same people were even sitting in the same chairs. The same people were squabbling and the same people were drunk. Even though I was only gone six weeks, for some reason, things seemed different, as far as my perception of things, that actually had not changed.

The next day I found a job, and went back to work within the next week. I was very thankful for that, because I had spent my savings and now had over $10,000 in debt. Unfortunately, I took a job that was a little over my head, skill wise, at the time, and after about three month's I felt ready for another vacation. But, I just switched jobs instead. I then went to work for Robert's Printing in Newton, Mass. This company gave me the money I wanted, full benefits coming in the door, and allowed me time off to have a surgery done that I had been putting off for over two years. I had to have a tumor removed from my Parotid saliva gland. I had the same surgery 7 years earlier and the tumor grew back. It was growing around all the nerves in my face. My smile, eyelid, and jaw were all affected, and painful. The surgery went well but my neck wasn't too pretty. I had a 6" incision from the top of my ear and a few inches down my neck. The first tumor was a golf ball sized mass, the regrowth was about the size of a grape. But the operation was not any simpler. But, considering that the doctor's warned me about the potential for facial paralysis, it was a great success.

It was soon after I arrived home from my trip that I began to change my lifestyle. I cut my drinking way back and stopped using other recreational substances. I was sick and tired of feeling sick and tired. I stopped going down the Elks so frequently. I also did some rethinking about other choices as well. I just started living a more boring, but safe lifestyle. My health got better, but my social life suffered. I think a lot of people would consider me a loner, but the fact is I love people, in small doses. But, I always love to see my nieces and nephews. It was at this time I became much more available for them and started taking them out a lot. As I got older (thirties) I just didn't go out much and looking back I spent an awful lot of time entertaining my brother's kids. But, no regrets. I called them my little friends, and we had a lot of fun times. I'm not sure how much of what I did was appreciated by their parents however, especially considering what has happened to those relationships since. But, I did it for the kids.

When Josh and Caleb were young. I was drinking a lot and I didn't take them out as often as Matt, Rob, Cassie, Mike and Sarah. But, I think I was still a pretty good uncle.

The motorcycle trip in 1990 was absolutely the best thing I have ever done. It made me feel like a better American, only because I knew the country better than ever before. I felt closer to God because when I saw the natural wonders of this world it just reaffirmed what I always believed. I think as a human being, that sometimes we get locked into our own little world, and we don't see the big picture, and all the people that are truly suffering right here in this country.

The plight of the Indians that I saw out west, and the poverty that they live in, really drives home the point for me, how unfair life can be. But, there are homeless and hungry right here in Massachusetts as well. I have had a good share of trouble in my life, and I know, that it is not very much that separates the comfortable (roof over my head, food to eat) life that I live, and the people who try to scrape out an existence. The circumstances and hardships, that the less fortunate have to endure, in many cases comes down to birth, and luck.

We are not all made of the same stuff, and mental illness, alcohol and drugs all take their toll on the less fortunate. I battle depression but I feel fortunate to be able to say I have never been hungry or homeless. I never had to ask for money from anyone except banks. I've always been able to repay my debts. My illness was a sobering dose of reality when I applied for free care at Brigham and Women's hospital to get my tumor treated. I was approved. If I had not been, I would probably be in tens of thousands worth of debt and most likely bankruptcy. I was also approved for disability by just sending them my records. The battle is not over but things don't get easier as you get older. My resume from 2002 on is spotty at best, with the exception of managing a rental property for 15 years. Honestly, I'm going to need a break because I'm no longer able to work in my trade and flipping burgers won't pay the bills. If it wasn't for my part time job managing a property, then I most likely would of been homeless. Thank God for that!

When you think of the poverty stricken and ill and then you come home and turn on the T.V., and all it is, is buy, buy, buy, and bigger, faster, newer. It just makes me question how much is enough.

Chapter Thirteen

What It Is

Please forgive me while I break from the format so far in the book, and record this day in time, on the day that me and my little buddy took a ride. This was several month's before my diagnosis, and my vision started to deteriorate rapidly not too long after I wrote this. I have not been able to hold a job, but at this time I was not sure why.

July fourth, 2003. Guess what, I'm unemployed, again, in a real tough economy and the money is running out. I'm almost 44, single, no kids. I have a lot of free time and that's why I'm writing this now. My bike is a 1977 BMW R100S. I like this bike and I hope I don't have to sell it. It needed a lot when I bought it, but I have it just the way I like it now (almost). It has a new top-end, clutch, rebuilt carbs, and new paint (gray). This is a cafe racer style machine and it was one of the fastest bikes on the road when it came out, but not for long, The Kawasaki kz bikes came right along. It handles excellent and has a very distinct sound and road feel. The opposed twin motor sounds, and feels, like no bike I have ridden before.

I woke up yesterday and the weather was beautiful. It was about 80 degrees, humidity was low, and the breeze was light. I decided to take one of my favorite rides, Gloucester Massachusetts. Gloucester is about thirty miles from my house. It's a working, fishing town. It was a weekday, so I didn't expect that much traffic down by the shore. I stopped by my brother's house before I left, and asked my nephew Michael if he wanted to go. He did. He's 10 years old.

We took off around 11:00 a.m., and got on route 128 north. We got off on route 22 north, and took that into Essex, where we stopped and had lunch at Farnham's Fried Clams, right on a marshy inlet out to the ocean. My nephew had French Fries, and an Iced Tea and I had a chowder and Iced coffee.

I took a route I knew, out to Gloucester Harbor, and we picked up Route 127 north. This road hugs the shore and the scenery is beautiful. There are numerous views of the rugged, rocky shore, and there are a few beaches along the way as well. Unfortunately, a lot of the coast is owned privately, and there is no access. There ought to be a law!

We stopped at an old granite rock quarry in the state park. The cliffs were over 50 feet straight down, and I suspect the water was very deep. There was no swimming allowed for obvious reasons. I would guess it was around 100 yards across and the shape was basically round.

My nephew seemed to really be enjoying himself, and he wanted me to keep moving. Route 127, and then route 127a will take you through Gloucester, and Rockport, and there are places for tourists to stop and spend their money, and the hungry to stop and eat.

We arrived back home around 4:30. It was a good ride and I can't think of a better way to spend a day.

Chapter Fourteen

The Longest Miles

Riding a motorcycle is a lot of fun, if your mind is in the right place. Sometimes, it's the last place you want to be. In July 1990, on my cross country trip, I called home and was told that my cousin Kenny had died. It hit me hard, and I had just had my little fender bender on the Wyoming and Montana border. From that point on, every mile seemed like ten, and every ache and discomfort was multiplied, I felt terrible. I wanted to be home with my family, but I was alone. Being alone at a time like this, is loneliness at it's worst. I had hoped that something like that would never happen again. Unfortunately, it did.

In 1994 I had a trip planned for Cape Breton, just north of Nova Scotia, and the Cabot Trail. This is roughly a two thousand mile ride, roundtrip. I was scheduled to leave the first of July.

At this time I was riding a 1994 Honda Pacific Coast. 800 c.c. It was a good bike, but it wasn't much to look at. It actually had a car style trunk. It was so easy to pack and unpack. But, it was a goofy looking machine. But, $4,800 dollars, brand new. It would do. It was a Honda, so I knew it would be dependable, and I had long rides in mind. It did have great road manners and was as quiet as could be.

About two weeks before I was going to go, I had gone to Maine with a couple of friends, and two of my cousins. My cousin Larry, and my cousin Jeff (better known as Biff). Larry had just split from his wife and he was in obvious pain.

Larry was someone I always looked up to growing up. When I was a kid. I don't think I was even 10, Larry asked me if I wanted to be "blood brother's", I said, yes, and asked him how. He stuck a needle in his thumb until he bled, and then my thumb, and we pressed them together. Jeff wouldn't do it. He said Larry was already his brother and I guess me and him being cousin's was close enough. When Larry had a fort in the woods he initiated me by letting a candle drip wax into my hands.

He was as strong as a bull, and everyone liked and respected him. One summer we were up in Maine and we were putting the raft in the water. Larry had made anchors by filling 5 gallon buckets with cement. He asked for help to put them in the water, but there was no way I could maneuver those things around, especially under water. Larry put his flippers on, and went into the water and placed all those anchors. He seemed to me, to be swimming while carrying these buckets of cement. I couldn't believe my eyes. I asked Larry, and he said, "I had flippers on" like it was no big deal. This *was* Larry.

On one occasion down the Elks a particular patron was giving Larry some lip, and Larry allowed it, for a while. Then he tossed the guy like he weighed 30 pounds. I said "Larry, you rag dolled him". He found that line amusing, and it would come up again, and again, over the years.

He could always drink a lot and he would amaze us with how much he could consume. When I was a teenager I saw nothing wrong with this. He once drank a case of beer in one night when he was about 18. Larry's favorite whisky was Wild Turkey.

Larry was a great guy, and a very hard worker. He took pride in the fact that he was stronger than most. He was tough as nails, and he never complained. He was always teasing me when I was kid. He said I was too sensitive and he tried to toughen me up. Once, I was complaining about something, and he just nonchalantly pulled up his pant leg and showed me his knee. It was swollen with fluid about the size of half a grapefruit.

He loved Clint Eastwood. Larry had some great facial expressions. He would curl one eyebrow and furrow his brow and give you a sideways glance and a growl. He had an alter ego, he named Vernon. You didn't want to bother Vernon.

He liked to doodle cartoons, and I always knew there was a lot under the surface that he wasn't revealing. He loved his mother. He loved his kids. He loved his dogs.

One time in Maine I wanted to fight my cousin Larry, and my cousin Abbott, at the same time. Alcohol was involved. I mentioned before that Larry thought I was too sensitive. I was. It didn't take that much to get to me. The two of them were pushing my buttons. So, I went outside, in a torrential downpour and challenged them both to come out. They just stood on the porch and laughed at me until I calmed down and came back in. It was over. No hard feelings.

Back to Larry's last weekend in Maine, he wasn't eating, and he was vomiting. He said he wasn't drinking (alcohol) and he was sleeping half the day, but I heard him up at night. I knew he was drinking. I was concerned, and I asked him what was going on. Who are you, my mother?, was his reply. I backed off.

He looked awful, and I smelled booze on him. He was having some deliriums. I felt helpless and so did Biff. He finally did eat a popsicle.

Shortly after returning home he ended up in the hospital. He was having liver trouble. It was hard to see him like this. He was still downplaying his condition. He assured me, that he was going to be all right, and, that after he got out of the hospital he was going into rehab. He told me I should go on my vacation, but I wasn't sure. I asked Biff, and he said that it was going to be a tough road, but he thought that his brother was going to get through this.

So, I followed through on my plans and went on my vacation. I was convincing myself the whole ride, that Larry was going to be all right. The weather was good, and Cape Breton was beautiful. This is the most beautiful place on the east coast. I've never been to to Ireland, but this is what The Cabot Trail reminds me of. The road hugs the mountains and the ocean simultaneously. The people here are very friendly, and original. They have a great sense of themselves and they do not seem to align themselves with the rest of Canada.

I was 800 miles away when I called home. Larry had died. I was shocked and heartbroken. I was told not to try and make the wake or funeral, because I was so far away. The wake was 24 hours away. There was no way I could make the wake, but I would try to make the funeral. I was already checked into a motel for the night, and I was in no condition to ride, besides the fact that the ferries would not be available. I would head for home at the crack of dawn or earlier.

I slept terrible that night. I was awake, packed and ready to go, long before the dawn. The weather was gloomy, cool, foggy, and light rain. After looking at my maps, I thought the best route, to make the best time, would be to drive the roughly 350 miles to Digby, and get the ferry for St. John. There are no major highways, and I would have to switch routes several times. By noon it was starting to rain and I wasn't making the best time. I tried a shortcut, and ended up getting off course, and setting myself back about an hour and a half. When I finally arrived at Digby the ferry was pulling away. I was too late. I would have to wait about two hours to get the next one.

After boarding the ferry, I went to my small cabin and caught a little sleep. I knew sleep would not be available again, until Massachusetts and home. I had five hundred miles or more left to travel, after reaching St. John.

A loud knock on the door woke me up, and I got ready to leave the boat. Now I thought I could make some time. I would take Route 1 south and pick up Route 9 in Calais, Maine. By this time it was raining heavily and I had to keep the speed reasonable, so much for making time.

As the light disappeared, I noticed a conspicuous absence of streetlights. The roads were very dark, winding, and dangerous. I was very tense and my hands gripped the bar as tight as I could. The muscles in my shoulders ached, and my boots were full of water. This was miserable, and I considered stopping. I thought my family would understand. Then, again and again, I would figure out in my head, how far, and how much time. I thought I could make it, so I kept going.

The visibility was absolutely horrible, the rain never let up, and it was windy, with strong gusts. From time to time, an eighteen wheeler would pass me, and the rush of air it created would push me. I would have to wipe my face screen over and over with my glove.

I finally hit Bangor, and route 95, around midnight. I thought from here it would get easier. But fatigue was setting in, and the weather wasn't improving. I was still 300 miles from home. One stretch of road along 95, was so straight and steady, I started to feel hypnotized by the streetlamps, and the lines of the road flashing by. I felt my eyes doze momentarily. That scared the hell out of me, and I did all I could to wake myself up, until I could stop.

I stopped at the next rest area. There was no shelter and it was still raining very hard. So, I laid down on a picnic table with my helmet still on, and

I immediately dozed off. I'm not sure how long, but a policeman woke me up with his flashlight. I was so physically, and mentally exhausted, and desperate for someone to talk to, I told him about Larry, and how I was trying to make it home for the funeral. He was kind to listen.

I drove all night and finally arrived home with enough time to sleep for three hours, and then go to the funeral. I was an emotional wreck, and when I was carrying the casket, I felt like I was going to collapse. It didn't seem real. It was a heartbreaking scene, with loved ones, and friends all paying their respects to a great person. This was a person that was in my life from day one. He was a cousin, and a friend. He was also my neighbor as a child. I could see his house if I looked over the fence in my back yard. I was over his house all the time. My Grandma was always there and she introduced me to ice tea and toast, congo squares, and fried dough. She would sing and play the piano. Her "stage name" was "Leonora".

I had dreams about Larry almost every night for a very long time. I stopped drinking entirely from this point on. I could not even stand to be around people drinking. My poor Aunt Alice, this was the second son she had lost in four years, and her husband died as well.

She had never recovered from the tragic losses of her sons. I think she blamed herself somehow, but those times (the sixties and seventies), had more to do with it than anything. Along with the fact that alcoholism, and other addictions seemed to run in our family.

It was the profound loss that I was feeling, that led me to church. I always believed in God, and that Jesus died for us and rose again. But I never fully, and completely sought him. I decided to go to "The Church of the Living God", where my sister Susan's husband was the pastor. I would bring my mother, and we would usually get together after church, with my sister Nancy and her family, or Susan and hers, or both.

The reason I left the church, was that I was suffering with depression. I eventually got help through modern medicine. I never believed that my depression had anything to do with demons. I believe it is somehow chemical related, but I can't explain, why I can have long stretches with no symptoms, and then it's like falling off a cliff. Everything slows down. I can't concentrate, my work suffers, etc.

With the death of my cousin Larry, came a lot of changes. No drinking, no drugs, and with me leaving the church and my earlier separation from my friends, I found myself somewhat isolated. Some family members, and especially children, were always there for me, and were always up for doing something. Especially, Cassie, Mike, Rob, and Matt, and Sarah.

BIFF'S COTTAGE

Chapter Fifteen

Bad News Good News

October 24, 2003. I had been having problems with my left eye for about two years. On this day I would find out why. I was scheduled for an M.R.I. at 8:30 a.m. It took about 40 minutes, and went well. I went home and almost immediately received a call from my doctor. It was a very large (4.5 cm or 1.8 in) pituitary tumor, and it was pressing on my optic nerves. She said it had to be removed as soon as possible or I could be risking permanent vision loss. I went and picked up the films from the M.R.I. and then went out to lunch with my mother and Aunt Alice. Then I went drinking.

I had lost 50 percent of my vision field in my left eye, and 25 percent in my right. I also lost color perception. Trying to continue in my field was impossible. I had been fired several times in the last three years. The doctor's I saw as my vision was going away were at a loss, as to why. One suggested I see a Psychiatrist. That was before I went to Brigham and Women's Hospital.

I had an appointment with a neurosurgeon in a couple of weeks and expected to have the operation very soon after that. His name is Peter Black and he is supposed to be the best in Boston, if not the world. My mother bought me a few things for my hospital stay.

Having this diagnosis was in some ways, a relief. Because, I felt so bad, for so long, and I was being doubted about my complaints. I have worked hard all my life, but because I was having so much trouble at this time keeping a job, one family member said, "he brings it on himself". Another thing that was said is "he should pull himself up by his bootstraps." These words hurt. My body was no longer producing testosterone and this brought many other symptoms. I felt so weak. My thyroid wasn't working properly either. But, I would have to toughen up.

November 1st. What a beautiful day. Clear skies and over 70 degrees. A perfect fall day for a motorcycle ride, but the truth is, I didn't want to ride anymore. With my vision problems, I felt extremely anxious driving, and didn't trust myself at all. I told my brother that I could no longer take his children in my truck. I was driving like an old lady, leaning forward, driving slow, and gripping the wheel with two hands. I was no longer able to read the paper easily and entire words would be missing due to a blind spot. I needed very bright light to be able to read at all. I watched a fight at my brother's house around this time, and it was a blur. My brother asked me if I was going to get a high definition t.v. and I told him I didn't have high def eyes.

As the days went by, I thought I was coming to terms with the operation coming up. I was worried but not scared. Who was going to pay for this, I didn't know. I had no insurance. I could be paying for it for the rest of my life, or it could be free. If.... I was approved for free care.

Most people that have this operation have their vision restored, if they act quickly enough. That's what I tried to focus on. Not, what if this, and what if that. Everything I do depends on good vision. Motorcycle riding, driving, photography, oil painting. My livelihood as well. Never mind looking at women. I was prayin' every day and I hoped the Lord would answer my prayers. Thanksgiving was coming up soon, and a lot of things were going to happen.

I never prayed harder, than the night after the follow-up with the doctor. She gave me medicine to shrink the tumor, and the side effects were awful. I was miserable. How this medicine worked would determine if surgery is still the best option. The tumor's size and the fact that it was extending into my cavernous sinus would make operating extremely difficult. So, the plan was to shrink the tumor some first.

The following morning I woke up and looked at the alarm clock. I could read it easily. I honestly felt that a miracle had happened. How could the medicine work so fast? Over the next three days my vision improved a lot. I could drive, and work, and read, and admire the sunset. Even the cloudy days seemed brighter.

For years things seemed dim to me. My thyroid problem was making cold air painful, and my testosterone deficiency made me feel weak, and my heart would pound climbing a flight of stairs. I also had gained 30 pounds. I started watching Lifetime movies. No joke.

In the following weeks, things were starting to look up, a lot. I got approved for free care at Brigham and Women's hospital. I had to wait and see what was next, as far as my condition and course of treatment but I was not nearly as concerned as I was three weeks earlier.

My financial situation was close to zero. I had $500.00 left to my name. The motorcycle was advertised for sale, but no bites. I had started to daydream a little once again. Looking past the winter and into the spring and working full-time. I would like to buy a new bike. The BMW R series boxer 1000. This bike is nice and only ten grand. What's money anyway, if you can't spend it on motorcycles. My next long trip? Who knows, but it's the riding that matters.

I started drinking again a little, and I have to admit I've been enjoying seeing some old friends. It's not quite the same as when I was young, but a couple of cold ones on occasion, is not going to hurt me. On Sunday, November 30, I had an MRI. to see how much the tumor has shrunk.

December 5th. I saw the doctor and learned that the tumor had shrunk 20 percent and that there would be no surgery for at least three months. There is a possibility that there will be no surgery at all, if.... I want to tolerate the side effects of the drugs and take them for the rest of my life. Their was also the fact that the medicine makes the tumor very hard, which would make removing it even more difficult. If the tumor stops responding to the medicine, then I will have a serious problem

Christmas and New Years had come and gone, and for the most part they were O.K., given the circumstances of my family relations. My brother Dickie's ex-wife Debra had a party on Christmas eve. Almost all the kids were there with the exception of my sister Susan's children and family. My brother Scott and his wife didn't attend, along with their daughter Sarah. My brother David and his wife didn't attend either. But all four of his girls were there.

There was Joshua and his girlfriend, Caleb, Matt, and Rob, from my brother Bob's family. Kate, Jesse, and sweet Ashley from my brother Dick's family. Cortney, Cristen, Shannon, and Raisa from my brother David's family. Jalyn, Zachary, Noelle, and Gabrielle, from my sister Nancy's family, and last but not least, Cassie and Michael from my brother Scott's family. The kids pulled it together this year, regardless of the family squabbling. It was really nice seeing them all. I love them so much. They grow up so fast. The girls are all beautiful and the boys are handsome. I'm not just saying that because they are my family. My siblings that attended were my brother Bob and his wife Maeva, Dickie was there, as well as Nancy and her husband Buddy. Of course my mother, the matriarch, Eunice Eva was there. She was always very generous at Christmastime.

The Christmas Eve traditional family party goes back to the mid seventies. Despite the problems this family has had, we have had a lot of good times together. The kids seem to appreciate their memories, and if the adults will grow up, this tradition can continue on. God willing.

As usual there is always a letdown after Christmas for me. This is when I'm acutely aware of my station in life. Still single, entering the dead of winter, and this year with health problems as well. I try to stay positive and appreciate the things I have, and the things we all have. Usually it is the thought of motorcycling and the spring that get me through.

I had been daydreaming a lot at this time, of a drive across country to the southern California coast. To Big Sur country. I would rent a motorcycle and travel a couple of thousand miles, just exploring. Time would tell if this would happen. But my last trip across country was preceded by the daydream. This daydream sees me solo again, or with one of my canine friends. Sort of like John Steinbeck in Travels with Charley.

Chapter Sixteen

Daydream

I've heard it said that you can't explain what motorcycling is, to someone that doesn't ride. To me, it's being far away from home, and away from all the stresses of work and family. The weather forecast is perfect, the bike is running great, and you have a 200-400 mile day mapped out. The excitement and anticipation of seeing, what you haven't seen before, is great.

The night before, you try to think of where you'll go, and what you'll see, and you get a rough idea with your maps and literature. If it's tourist season, you have to get up with the crack of dawn, or risk just being another tourist, stopping at all the same places, and riding along in traffic. Which negatively effects the experience.

So, it's around 5:a.m., and and my travel alarm goes off. I know the forecast is good, and there's a lot to see. Usually, I jump in the shower. But, the truth is I don't always shower daily on the road. I start to pack, and do my inventory. The way I pack the bike is the exact same way every single time. So, that when I want something, I can find it.

It's a cool 50 degrees outside and the bike is covered with dew and you can see your breath, the earthy smell of the forest is in the air. The first couple of hours will be chilly, but well worth it. I'll wipe the bike down, check the oil, and warm up the bike.

The packing usually takes about 1/2 hour. Check everything one last time, put on my gloves and goggles, swing my leg over (which isn't always easy), put up the kickstand, fire up the bike, look around, put it in gear, release the clutch, twist the throttle and go. And off to another adventure.

The first priority, once I'm out of the motel and moving, is to stop, eat, and have coffee. When you're on the road, this isn't always nearby. So, sometimes you have to settle for what you can find at a gas station. It will probably be 9:a.m. before I find something good. So, a coffee, cold drink, and Drakes pastry will be fine until then.

The orange glow of the sun is coming up from the east, and gently burning off the fog. Getting out there early, you have the added advantage of seeing wildlife.

My favorite ride, and what I'm thinking about as I write this, is Skyline Drive in Virginia. It really is a great part of the country. The sun starts to warm you up as it peaks through the trees. You wind your way down the road and you notice that there is no commercialism, no gas stations, no signs, nothing but 150 miles of forest and Skyline Drive carving through The Shanendoah National Forest. This time of morning, there is almost no-one on this road. That all changes later. That's why no matter where I travel, this is the time of day I like to be on the road. You can feel the nature, and admire the beauty. If you don't ride too fast or make too much noise, you should see lots of deer.

You'll feel the cool wind in your face, your eyes will tear, and the wind will noisily pass around your ears. The cold air going down the back of your collar, can sometimes chill you to shivers. But,.....This is living.

When afternoon rolls around, and the thought of rest and food is starting to outweigh the thought of moving on, I start to think of stopping. The budget always rules here. When I travel, I try to spend less than $50.00 a night. On rare occasions I'll break out the plastic and pamper myself with a $80.00 to $100.00 a night hotel, and a great steak dinner and drinks in the hotel bar. Almost always there are friendly people that will strike up a conversation with the stranger.

Chapter Seventeen

Dogs

Because I've written about all the things that have brought me some great times and memories, I think there is one more thing that I would like to write about. Dogs. Dogs are great! Why, you ask? They will never lie to you, or put on a front. If they seem happy to see you, they are happy to see you. They will never repeat something you said. They will always be there for you when you call. They will defend you when under attack. They don't hold grudges. They will never question your motives. If you are taking them for a walk, that is all they need to know. They will never say mean hurtful things to you, or about you. They *will* take advantage if you let them, *so*, if that happens, that's *your* fault. They have an amazing capacity for love!

My early years I felt a bit like Tom Sawyer. A trip to Dike's pond, the woods, the tower, were all nearby and available to me. I had a lot of freedom as a kid, and my imagination and curiosity kept me occupied and happy, and there were always dogs included.

My earliest memories are of a big boxer in the neighborhood, I was about four. I just remember how happy, patting that dog, made me feel. He was not a healthy looking dog, and my father didn't like that he would come in the yard.

Then there was Sandy. My Aunt Alices's dog. She was a small mixed breed, spaniel and retriever, I think. She loved to hunt, and was always bringing mice home. That dog loved me, and she was always showing up on my back porch looking for me. Every summer I would go to Maine to my Aunt Alices's cottage with my cousin's Jeff and Larry. My Aunt "Al" had a big Ford Galaxy 500, and Sandy would ride up on the back deck, and her hair would be whipping around the whole way. Sandy had a best friend in Maine. His name was Skipper. They were like a newly married couple. Where there was one, there was the other. They loved each other. It was hard to see Sandy get old, and she never seemed the same after another dog was brought home. Lia was a German shepherd with a bad disposition. A good dog, but cranky, and she definitely dominated Sandy.

I finally got my own dog in 1970. My father took me out to the Buddy dog humane society kennel in Sudbury Mass., to adopt a dog. We walked in, and there was an immediate racket of dogs barking, and we walked from cage to cage, looking at each one.

There was a Husky that looked absolutely perfect to my father. He was big and strong, and was wagging his tail, and licking my hand. That was the one that my dad wanted. But we continued down the row of cages, and we came to this small cage with a dog back in the corner. She was brown and furry, with long hair covering her eyes, and the cage was so small she couldn't sit all the way up. Her name was Peanut Butter. She looked sad, and nervous. I wanted her, and my dad said okay. I couldn't of been any happier, and once Peanut Butter was in the car with us, she was happy too. I changed her name to Cocoa. When we arrived home, my family was in the living room, and Cocoa was out her mind excited, jumping from lap, to lap, in absolutely crazy excitement.

Unfortunately, Cocoa's time with us was cut tragically short. It happened on a Saturday morning. I was coming home from C.C.D. with my little sister. I wanted to go see if Dike's pond was frozen, my sister wanted to go with me, but, I said no, and when we reached the corner of my street, I told her to go home. When I was walking home from Dike's, my brother Bobby came to stop me. He had picked Cocoa up off the street. She was dead, and he placed her in one of my father's cardboard boxes, that he used for bread. He tried to stop me from going to her, but I did anyway and I lowered my head to hers. She was very bloody. She was run over and killed in front of my house on December 5th, 1971. We only had her for seven month's. I was heartbroken. I never cried as hard, or for as long as I did when I lost her. I was 12 years old, but I cried for hours while clutching rosary beads. We buried her in the back yard, and I made her a cross. I never wanted another dog. I've thought of her every December fifth since then.

But against my wishes, a dog was brought to me in late January. She was a tiny little thing. She was the runt of the litter, and was rejected by her mother. We had to feed her with a baby bottle. We named her Cappy.

Cappy was my dog, and I loved her. I did everything for her. I trained her and brushed her, and played with her, constantly. She was a Godsend. There was a lot of turmoil in my house growing up. It was a nut house a lot of the time, but Cappy seemed to sense when I was low, and she would stay right by my side. She slept with me most of the time, but she also liked to sleep next to my dad on the living room couch, or in my brother Scott's bed.

She was absolutely obsessed with playing with a ball. It was non-stop all day. If someone would throw it, she would go get it. My poor mother couldn't even sit in the yard without Cappy repeatedly giving her the ball, and then barking until she would throw it.

She was part terrier and part poodle, gray and black, about 25 pounds with long hair over her eyes. In the summer we would give her a poodle cut. She looked like a different dog.

It was absolutely amazing to me that she would find a ball no matter where we went. One time I took her down to the pine forest. There was a field next to the forest with grass over a foot tall. I had one of my friends cover her eyes, and I threw the ball as far as I could, and then set her loose to find it. She would run straight out, and then start hopping, similar to how an Impala does. She seemed to use logic, ruling out, one zone, after the other. If I called her name, she would stop and look directly at me, and I could point in any direction and she would immediately move to the area I was pointing. Even if it was thirty yards to my left and she was 50 yards in front of me to the right. After finding the ball she would come prancing back to me as though she was a proud pony.

One day I threw the ball and it ended up going over the neighbors fence. I went into the house, and I was standing in the kitchen looking out the back door, when I saw her leap right over the fence without touching it. The fence was four feet tall. This would turn out to be her claim to fame. She would definitely impress all the kids who saw her.

CAPPY

As she got older she would jump and land on top of the fence, and then go over. One day her leg got stuck and she tore her tendons. She needed an operation or she was basically going to be a three legged dog. We had it done. It was $350.00. I paid half, and my father paid half. I was seventeen. Cappy was seven. She recovered beautifully and was back to her old ways in no time.

I got thrown out of the house when I was eighteen, but I didn't take Cappy with me. I would still stop by and visit frequently. My mother did my laundry for a while after I moved out, and my father would make Sunday dinner.

We were reunited in 1984 when my brother Scott and I rented a house together. My parents were selling their house and my father asked me if I would give up my apartment so that I could get one to share with my brother. Cappy was getting old by this time. She had lost most of her hearing and her eyes were going bad too. She could no longer control her bladder. But it was great having her with me again. I liked living with my brother too. Even though he could be a real pain in the ass.

We moved into another house in 1985, and took on two more roommates, one of which was my cousin Biff (Jeff). One roommate wanted Cappy kept in the garage when we weren't home. In retrospect we should of put him in the garage. Late that year, we were talking about what we were going to to when the lease was up. We decided we were all going to go our separate ways. I anguished over what to do with Cappy. She was suffering and and her health was failing. But, she was still capable of giving and receiving love. Cappy was fourteen. I decided to have her euthanized.

I brought her to the vet. She had been there before but she never reacted like this. It was as if she knew. She wet the floor and wrapped her two front legs around my leg and squeezed, so tight, and cried. I couldn't do it, and we left. It was awful. Six months later I decided it had to be done.

I had stupidly broken my right hand during the 1985 Super bowl between the Pats and Da' Bears. We had a party at the house, and it got out of control. I stupidly punched the refrigerator. Consequently I lost my job.

I decided to take a ride to Florida. My brother Scott decided he would like to come with me. I was glad. I had made an appointment to have Cappy "put to sleep" while we were gone. I asked my Mother if she would do it for me. She did, along with my sister Nancy. I had terrible guilt about this for years. I just wished she could of died a natural death, and that I could of buried her. In the Pine Forest maybe.

Chapter Eighteen

M + M's + Coffee

The trip to Florida with my brother was memorable in a lot of ways. There was the fact that I had lost my job, due to my broken hand, and Cappy was gone, and then the trip itself. It was a spur of the moment type of thing, with no planning and very little money. My father lent us his 1985 Delta 88 for the ride.

This trip was fueled by gasoline, m&m's and coffee. I drove most of the way, one stretch driving a thousand miles straight. Scott slept through most of that. He would poke his head up from time to time, from the back seat, and ask, "where are we" and "when are we going to eat?" I still remember one meal at the Cracker Barrel, and the really cute waitress that waited on us.

I had been down south previously a couple of times to travel Skyline Drive and the Blue ridge Parkway. These two roads (same road, two states) combined would take you 600 miles through some of the best scenery, and the best motorcycling roads you could ever ride. That's what we were planning to do. I had never done it in the winter, but I knew it was only under extreme conditions that the road would close. Guess what. The conditions were bad, and the road was closed, due to a huge snowstorm. We had to stop at the nearest motel, and there was no working heat. We had peanut butter and some snacks to eat, and that was it. We watched the "Brother from another planet" and stayed under our blankets. We couldn't wait at this point to get to warm weather.

Once again, my circumstances would be the same when I got home, but the fact that I was on the road, and heading south, was improving my mood by the mile. You could feel the winter melting away by the hour. We had a lot of music with us and Scott was doing a good D.J. job...., when he was awake.

We only got as far as the gulf coast, but that was fine. We stayed in Panama City. The weather was good and the hotel was nice. It was right on the shore. It had it's own bar and I settled right in for a couple of drinks. We went out for a meal (mussels and beer) and played some pool. It was a sleepy little town. But there was a bar with music. I went out and got drunk that night. Scott stayed at the hotel.

In less than 24 hours we were heading home. We were passing through Mobile, Alabama, when I noticed a bar, went in, and had a couple of beers and talked to the locals. Scott eventually woke up and noticed the car wasn't moving and came in. They had a good Juke box.

Further on up the road, in Georgia, after a torrential downpour, we would see submerged homes off the side of the highway. We drove through Atlanta just for the heck of it. It was about 1:a.m. and the town was dead.

Nothing especially exciting or new happened on this trip but it was still fun. I hope to get back to Florida and drive the Keys by motorcycle some day, and I would like to see the Everglades National Park.

Chapter Nineteen

The South

The south has drawn be back, again and again. My first trip was Skyline Drive, and then The Blue Ridge Parkway, and then a trip in a Winnebago, with my brother Scott and some friends. On that trip we drove Skyline Drive, and then went to Virginia Beach. That ride was just a party on wheels.

Several years later, it was the solo trip to New Orleans. Two weeks on the road, heavy rain every day, except for the 24 hours I spent in New Orleans. I mentioned earlier a few of the things that happened in that 24 hour period. But there is one aspect of the trip that bares mentioning. The scammers are everywhere and you have to watch your back, as if your safety depended on it. One scam was the "Shoeshine Boss?", scam. A group of kids would approach you, get on all sides, and offer to shine your shoes. If you accept, they will wait for the opportune moment and grab and run, or they will demand an unreasonable amount of money after they begin to shine. I declined, and tried to keep moving but they pursued me for a whole block, until I got on to Bourbon Street.

I was probably perceived to be an easy mark. I was alone, obviously a tourist, and I was carrying expensive camera equipment. I was not yet drunk though. After putting the camera away, and going down to Bourbon Street, I was approached by a young black man, offering me a free line of Cocaine. I think his idea was to get me into an alley to do it, and then rob me. I declined over and over, but this kid wouldn't leave me alone. Finally, I did go into that alley and I don't even know what I snorted. What an idiot I was to put myself in such a situation. After leaving the alley I offered to buy him a drink. We went into a bar, and he went to the bathroom. The barmaid knew immediately that I was from out of town, and warned me that this kid was bad news. After we had our drink, he offered to repay the favor by buying me a drink, at a bar he knows. I accepted.

The Outback section of New Orleans is not for tourists. It was about a ten minute walk out of the French Quarter (I had no idea at the time). We got to a bar and I was pretty buzzed by this time, and I was up for anything. The place was packed, and loud. Entering the club, every single step to the bar was difficult, due to the overcrowding. But, the crowd was not cooperating with me either. By the time I reached the bar, I realized I was the only white person in the place. When I stepped up to the bar, the bartender put his arms on the bar, leaned forward and looked me sternly in the face. "What are you doing in here?", he asked me. He refused to serve me and suggested that I leave.

I could not wait to get out of there, and it took me a while (it seemed), as the crowd didn't seem to be cooperating with my leaving either. The guy that brought me, was right on my trail, and I was starting to think I was being set up. I did get safely back to the relative security of the French Quarter, before we went our separate ways. Looking back I realize, to go there, with him, wasn't too bright.

The music of New Orleans, and the South in general is a large part of the attraction for me. New Orleans is mainly known for the jazz, Memphis is known for the blues, and bluegrass is a southern music. I had the opportunity (time and money) to travel there with a friend in 1992. We rented a big Lincoln Town Car, and set off to see Graceland and to party on Beale Street.

If you ever want to test a friendship, a four thousand mile road trip by automobile is a good test. The littlest things can get on your nerves after a while. On a bike, you're out there in the wind. In a car, the confinement can get to you, at least it did me.

But the car was beautiful, we had plenty of cash, and the weather was good. This was the first time for Joe to see the south. We took the back roads across Kentucky and this was the most memorable and scenic part of the trip. There was a light rain, and the grass was as green as could be. We passed a lot of Stables and we saw some beautiful horses along the way.

We had an agreement about drinking in the car. We wouldn't do it. If you knew Joe, you would understand why I asked that we not drink in the car. Joe loves beer. I was doing most of the driving and Joe was picking the music. We had the Beer all packed in Ice in the trunk. We were thirsty but there were many miles to go before we would drink. Every time we stopped, Joe would make sure the beer had plenty of ice.

We didn't have an itinerary for Memphis but there were a couple of things we wanted to do. Beale Street, Graceland, and The Rendezvous for the ribs.

After checking into our Hotel, we took the two block walk down to Beale and immediately went into B.B. Kings bar. The drinks were great, and so was the music. Joe settled in on a bar stool, and decided that was where he was going to spend the night. I went exploring. One cover charge, would get you into every bar on Beale. I think I had, at least a drink, in almost all. I went back to B.B.'s place and found Joe, before we staggered our way home.

Graceland was interesting and fun. I'm not a huge Elvis fan, but you can't deny his influence on music. The glass cases at Graceland, full of Elvis's stuff, was what I liked the most. I would of expected the place to be a little bit more luxurious than it was. The upstairs was off limits the day we were there but we got to see the Jungle room.

Another must see if you're a music fan in Memphis, is Sun Records. This is where Elvis, Johnny Cash, Carl Perkins, and anybody else in the area back in the fifties, would get studio time, or make records. We were tight on time, so after having our ribs at the Rendezvous, we set off for home.

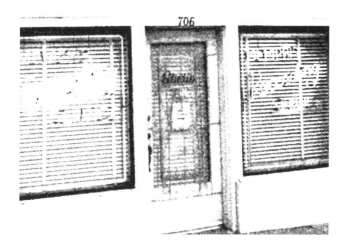

SUN RECORDS

The place that most people think of, when they think of music and the South, is of course Nashville, Tennessee. Music City, U.S.A.. The year that I traveled there wasn't for the music exactly, although I did get my share in the seedier side of town. Namely, Printers Alley. It's not what it used to be, but if you want to hear some country music by some young musicians trying to break in, or by some long time gone by musicians, trying to stay in, you'll find it here, along with some of the grimier side of an American city.

Nashville is the starting point of The Natchez Trace Parkway. I read about it in a motorcycle magazine, and before I knew it I was on my way. The reaction of the people I told that I was going, was utter bemusement. Like, why would anyone want to go to Mississippi, in July? For me the reason was clear before I started, and even clearer after I drove it. It is simply one of the most enjoyable motorcycling roads in the United States.

It starts In Nashville and travels Southwest, almost 500 miles across Tennessee, Alabama, and Mississippi, and ultimately ends on the shore of The Mississippi River in Natchez Mississippi. It runs roughly along the course of The Old trace.

This was all once Indian land, like of the rest of our country. The Choctaw, Chickasaw, and most likely Cherokee, all inhabited this area. The trace began as simple footpaths that the indians would travel in their daily lives. History has the old trace dated back to 1300.

The first outsiders to arrive in the area were the French in 1716. The Indians began trade, and allowed the encroaching civilization to use their paths. Then came the British and Spanish. In 1798 The United States gained control of the area.

The main use of The Trace, was primarily to walk home, after cities up river would float their goods downstream to Natchez, or New Orleans for trade. These are the days before steamboats, and the only way home was to walk. This was not an easy journey because there were bandits and outlaws along the way, waiting to take advantage of any opportunity that presented itself. The traveler of this time would encounter Frontier people, Settlers, Traders, Soldiers, Post riders, Backwoodsmen, Boatmen, and of course Indians.

The Boatmen of reputation were called Kaintucks. A name synonymous with "rough and rowdy". Andrew Jackson once said, " I never met a Kaintuck that didn't have a rifle, a deck of cards, and a bottle of whisky". The Steamboat was invented in 1811, essentially ending the Kaintucks colorful influence over the area.

F.D.R. and the New Deal in the 1930's, began the construction of The Natchez Trace Parkway as we know it today. A 500 mile ribbon of pavement through some of the most beautiful and unspoiled countryside this country has to offer. There is a 50 M.P.H. speed limit the lentire ength of the Trace. There are no billboards, commercial vehicles, stop lights, or any sign of modern times. The silence is amazing when you pull off and listen, with the exception of birds. Which there are many, and they all have songs and colors that I didn't recognize from the North.

I passed swamplands, deep woods, ridges, bottom lands and meadows. I saw archaeological sites dating to 1300. There was one Indian burial mound that took up eight acres. I got off the Trace and had a catfish and grits lunch one day. It was just *o.k.* I visited an old church deserted in the woods. But most of all, I rode 500 miles one way, of gentle sweeping, mesmerizing road. The best part was, I would get to ride it again on the way back.

I ended up at Natchez Under the Hill. This was once a renowned drinking place for all the characters mentioned above, that passed this way.

I decided to spend the night in Natchez and go drinking. I made some friends that night. I played pool and darts, and got into a "discussion" about the Civil War. I ended up getting a couple of guys there quite aggravated, and angry with me. My new friends got me out of there just in time. I think those guys were about ready to kick my ass. When we left, they came outside, and we pulled away.

There are two places in the south that are above all the rest for me. One for it's natural beauty and civil war history. The other for the sheer magnitude of an historical civil war event.

Harpers Ferry, West Virginia, sits where the Potomac and Shanendoah Rivers converge. The town also sits just across the river from both Maryland and Virginia. The first time I traveled there was by motorcycle, and I was struck by all the things that this little town had. The rivers and the surrounding Blue Ridge Mountains, historical sites, quiet little streets, and good people. The view from in front of The Hilltop House Hotel is just beautiful. You sit high on a hill, overlooking the rivers, and there is a train trestle that crosses over the river. You would think that this is the best view in town, but if you climb the 1448 foot Maryland heights, the view is simply amazing. You can see the whole lower town, and out across the rivers and their mountainous backdrop.

Before the Civil War, this was the home of a Federal Garrison and Armory, due to it's strategic location.

The fact that there were all these weapons here caught the attention of an Abolitionist by the name of John Brown. He set off to seize the 100,000 weapons with his "Army of Liberation" on October 16, 1859. His mission was to free the slaves, and create a slave uprising. He succeeded in capturing the garrison and other key spots in town. But the battle would be short-lived. Thirty six hours later, after most of his men were killed, Brown was captured in the firehouse when the U.S. Marines stormed the building. Brown was hanged by the neck on December 2, 1859. The country was headed toward Civil War. John Brown died for what he believed in. During the war, Harper's ferry would change hands eight times between the north and the south.

The Hilltop House is absolutely gorgeous, and would deserve the trip here on it's own. The lodging, the views, and the food, are excellent. I've stayed overnight here twice. Once with my brother Scott, and once with my friend Joe, on our trip to Memphis. The building is over 150 years old at this writing, and has provided lodging for Mark Twain, Alexander Graham Bell, and Woodrow Wilson.

There is another place in the south, as I mentioned. That place is Antietam (Sharpsburg). Of course if you've traveled in the south at all, you will cross many places that Civil War history has taken place, but no place affected me like Bloody Lane in Antietam.

On September 17, 1862, the North and the South converged, for an epic battle that would leave 22,000 men dead, wounded, or missing. It was, and is, to this day, America's bloodiest day. This was the first Civil

War engagement in the north, and a turning point in the war. According to eyewitnesses, Robert E. Lee's army was ruined, and the Confederacy had little time left.

When I traveled there, and stood on that site, and tried to imagine what had happened there, it got to me. Bloody lane is an 800 yard lane that had been worn deep by wagons. This is where the rebels tried to make their stand. They fought back Union charges four times. The battle raged for three and a half hours. This battle gave Lincoln the victory he badly needed, and shortly thereafter President Lincoln issued "The Proclamation for Emancipation". Freeing the slaves.

This battle created an immediate crisis, that had everyone scrambling to get the dead buried, and the wounded treated. One farm buried seven hundred men. Sharpsburg became a Hospital with all available space and resources given over to the task. In 1864, land was purchased for permanent burial sites. The wounds between the north and south, were too fresh to bury Rebel and Union soldiers together, so there were separate graveyards. The task of exhuming and reinterring these men was monumental. The bodies were identified by letters, photographs, diaries, or markings on the soldiers belt, or ammo box. 60% of the men were buried as unknowns.

I was there in the middle of summer. The surrounding area is beautiful and the roads are great for riding. But, "progress"(malls) is closing in, and changing the south for good. I would later travel to Gettysburg, but it was so overrun with tourists that the experience was not even close to Antietam.

Chapter Twenty

Gratitude and Goodbyes

In June 2004, we were helping my mother, doing final preparations for her move into her new apartment. I was hanging pictures for her, and setting up her fishtank. I was not well at the time, as I was dealing with my illness and the affects of my medication. I was weak, dizzy, irritable and depressed. I was glad for my mother though, as she was very excited about moving into her new apartment.

On August 12, my brother Dickie called my mother. She was only able to answer the phone, because she collapsed next to the bed. She told my brother she was o.k. but he knew better and called 911. She was having a major stroke.

The next year was extremely difficult, as my mother was having terrible difficulty with swallowing, and she lost the use of her left side. She was living in the Winchester Nursing Center, but we all gave my mother hope that she could still recover and return home. Many days, she would ask when she was going home, I would always tell her "not today ma, just rest today", and she would calm down most times.

My mother had changed a lot due to the stroke, and she was often confused. She thought my father was still alive on many days, and I would have to tell her over and over that he was gone. She would have great adventures in her dreams, and she would travel far and wide, and would tell everybody where she had gone. But, she thought she had really done these things. My mother cried so much. I would just hold her hand and let her cry. She would sometimes say, that she thought she was not a good mother, and I told her that she was. She was always there, and she did the best she could.

She had congestive heart failure as well, which would prove a major challenge. She said numerous times that she wished that she had died, and she was afraid that her family was going to forget about her in there. I promised her I would visit every day, and that I would get her out of there as often as I could. We bought a wheelchair van, and upgraded her wheelchair due to her terrible discomfort with the one provided.

Our mother continued to lose weight over the next year, as she was only able to swallow about 25% of what she tried to swallow. Eunice's inability to easily swallow her medications, especially the high blood pressure medication, caused many crises. The nurses repeatedly recommended that she get a feeding tube, but she was reluctant, as all of us were. Eunice was a fighter though, and worked very hard at rehab and therapy. She was the favorite of almost everyone there, because she had such a great sense of humor, and her genuine interest and compassion with the people there. She referred to her aides as her angels. Especially Rosalyn, and Delette. Eunice was the kindest and most thoughtful person I have ever known. She would remember the birthday's of all her children, and grandchildren, and friends. She helped me remember too.

Before the stroke our mother was a worrier. She always chewed her nails, and would always wait for her children to come home from school, while sitting at the base of the stairs and looking out the window.

When I told her some of the things I did as a child while off adventuring she said she had no idea. She allowed me my freedom and it was a simpler time back then.

At Christmastime in 2006 my mother asked me what was the favorite gift that I ever received. I told her it was the excitement, and anticipation of Christmas, and how I was always happy on Christmas morning. She said "that was a good answer".

My parents went all out at Christmas. The tree, the decorations, all the cards all taped up. My father would play his Christmas records. There was lots of food, and fun, and love. They bought us all so much stuff. It was overwhelming coming down the stairs on Christmas morning and seeing it all. I don't have a single bad memory of Christmas as a kid. It was great!

My mother was a contradiction when it came to money. On the one hand she would be frugal, and sensible, when it came to her own needs. She would say that she had lived through the Great Depression, and this experience obviously afffected her. I would always tell her to "spend it ma", "take a trip, or buy yourself something". She would say, "I don't need anything". She saw how I spent money, and used credit cards and she would always tell me about "all that interest", and that I should "save for things I wanted". But with her children that were in need, she would help. Or, when asked she would lend. I would help my mother so that she could have it a little bit easier. Especially with her expenses over the Christmas holiday. She was very grateful.

In April 2005 it was clear that my mother would not survive much longer without proper nutrition, and medicine, she decided to have the feeding tube. She bravely held her ground, as there were differing opinions on this. It saved her life, and as she got stronger, she started doing much better swallowing, and she seemed to start enjoying her life. Food was always very enjoyable for my mother, especially sweets, and now she could enjoy them again. She did not like the nursing home food however, and when I would ask how it was, she would make a sour face.

In November 2005, I would be tested. My mother was put in the unfortunate circumstance, of having to choose one son, over another, to handle her health, and carry out her wishes, after she passed. To put it as delicately as I can, this meant there was a lawyer involved, and my name was removed as the executor.

At this time, I was working, running a six color press on the overnight shift. This press was 8' tall and roughly 30' feet long. I worked from 5:00 p.m. to 5:00 a.m., and I arrived at the nursing home every day to help my mother eat breakfast at 10:00 a.m. I would come back to help her with lunch at noon, and then I would try to take a nap before going to work.

My employer, would not give me health insurance, because of my pre-existing condition. I was also trying to run a broken down press, by myself, on the overnight shift. Presses this large are usually a three man job. The head pressman would be responsible, and make all decisions, the second pressman would assist the pressman, and the feeder, would load the paper.

I was under a great deal of stress at this time, and I was battling the worst insomnia of my life. Many nights I was arriving for a 12 hour shift, with only 4 hours of sleep the previous night. Something had to give. I asked for help from my siblings but they were unavailable to help.

When I learned that I was removed as the executor, I was overwhelmed. I didn't visit my mother for three days. Looking back, I'm glad that I forgave my mother so quickly, and resumed what I was doing. My mother depended on me.

My problems at work, got worse, however. Everything came crashing down, when I fell, unconscious, on my kitchen floor. I had no idea how long I was out for. I called my doctor the next morning, He instructed me to go to the emergency room. They did a spinal tap, because they thought that the tumor might be leaking. It wasn't. They could not explain what happened.

I was not comfortable trying to run this machine any longer, if I could not be sure that I would not pass out again. I was also exhausted and depressed and I needed to try and get my sleeping problems and my depression under control. I never went back to work there.

One year later I casually mentioned to my mother, how much her actions hurt me. She was confused. She said that she *did make my brother executor*, but she *never took anything away from me*. She said she would never do anything that would hurt me. I believed her.

My mother mentioned many times, how grateful she was for the extra time that she was blessed with. She got to attend the weddings of two of her grandchildren. She attended Christen's wedding to John, and Joshua's wedding to Josephine. We got her out on the holidays, and she attended get together's at Bobby's, Dickie's and Susan's houses. I would take her to Gloucester, and the Charles river, and Lexington, and out for ice cream, and to look at the Christmas lights, and to the movies. I am so grateful for the time I got to spend with my mother, and that I had the opportunity to show her how much I loved her.

Scott's daughter Cassie was hit by a car, and almost died in June of 2006, and was miraculously resuscitated at the scene of the accident by an off duty policeman, that by the grace of God, witnessed the accident. Cassie is my Goddaughter, and we always had a good relationship. I love her dearly. My mother would tell the story, and would refer to it as *a miracle* that she survived.

My mother lost her sister Alice, and she got to attend her wake. My Aunt Alice was wonderful to my mother, and to me. I spent so much time at her house growing up. She lived on the next street, and she had three son's named Kenny, Larry, and Richard Jeffrey(Jeff). Me and Jeff were best friends growing up and we spent a lot of time together in the 70's and 80's. We drank, used drugs, and drank some more. We listened to a lot of music and our musical tastes were very similar. Frank Zappa, Rory Gallagher, Roy Buchanan, Jeff Beck, Black Sabbath, The Who, ZZ Top, and dozens of other's.

After Jeff lost his brother Larry, we didn't see much of each other, since I had quit drinking, and he got married. I wasn't aware of the extent of his drinking until my Aunt Alice's death. Unfortunately Jeff succumbed to alcoholism in 2008. The whole family was now gone. Uncle Kenny, Kenny (aka Harry), Larry, Aunt Alice, and then Jeff (aka Biff).

Eunice Eva Stockbridge died on July 27th of 2007 after a lengthty and courageous battle. I miss her dearly, and think of her daily. Rest in Peace Ma.

AUNT ALICE, UNCLE JACK, AND MA

Chapter Twenty One

Brody And Me

In June of 2008, I was at my most recent job for two years. I had hurt my neck, and after month's of physical therapy, epidural spine injections, and month's of short term disability, I was unable to return to work due to the heavy lifting involved.

There was a betrayal by a close family member while I was going through this very difficult time. I became depressed and stopped attending church. I was feeling hopeless. My brother even asked me if I was thinking of "cashing in my chips". I have battled depression most of my life, with major mood swings. This has been a major obstacle, in regards to work, and relationships. I have always been honest about this, but unfortunately, from some, this has brought either mocking, or blame. But sometimes anger is justified!

I was driving one day and I came across a 1985 Chevrolet conversion van, hightop, with a sleeping compartment. The owner was asking $1,700. I decided to buy it. There is only one reason I wanted to buy it.*"To drive cross country, and to get away from here."*That's two reason's!

I was talking to my nephew Matthew, and I mentioned my crazy idea about driving cross country. He said I should get a dog. I was thinking the same thing. That very day I looked in the Boston Herald and found an ad for an Australian Shepherd. His name was Brody.

I went to meet him and he was terrified of me, and he had some definite trust, and fear isssues. I bought him.

In less than two weeks we were on the road, for a one month, 8,000 mile journey. I could not afford this trip, I would be charging the majority of the expense, and I hoped to figure things out when I returned.

This dog was a major handful from day 1, and we had a major battle of wills for the entire trip. But, I saw gradual improvements and I felt that he just had to learn that, *I, was his, best friend.*

We saw the country together, and he made me laugh every day. He can be the goofiest, most loveable dog. Every experience was brand new for him and I loved watching his reactions. Especially to wildlife. He goes bananas!

We saw Badlands National Park, Yellowstone, Yosemite, Seqouia, and Kings Canyon. We went to Monterey and drove route 101. We saw so much wildlife on this trip. We saw buffalo, elk, coyote, hundreds of deer, mules, and wild turkeys. I even saw a mother bear and her cubs, in North Carolina's beautiful Smoky Mountain National Park, after taking Route 40 across the country, and back home from California. We came upon a bear jam (traffic stopped because of a sighting), I jumped out of my van and climbed up an embankment to try and get a look, and when I got to the top, Momma bear was about 20 feet away and she gave us brief charge in our direction before turning and running away with her cubs. Driving across the desert in Nevada was unreal, and somewhat unnerving, as we took a two lane backroad with almost no traffic and no services for 100 miles. Yosemite was amazing. Absolutely Amazing! Especially Glacier Point. John Muir was right.

The first day on the road was the longest it seemed. I had tears streaming down my face, more than once. It seemed like so many things were flooding my mind. Especially my mother. But also the loss of someone that I always trusted, and now realized the relationship was over as I knew it. I will forgive and I hold out hope that I will be apologized to, but it has now been over a year. It hasn't happened. My relationship with my family has never been worse. Most of the damage was done over differences of opinion over the care of my mother. Such as the feeding tube and numerous other things. I only backed up what my mother wanted at *ALL times*. I've spoken my mind a few times too, and this brought consequences as well. I have no regrets. I was tired of being lied to.

I was once drawn in from many people about concerns over one of my nieces. Everybody felt that something had to be said. I made the mistake of putting my nose in and it created a terrible mess and I ended up taking all the heat. I apologized but I have never been forgiven. I feel that this episode brought on a lot of the difficulty I was subjected to during my mother's illness. I would just ask, please, just listen to the facts, and ignore the gossip and rumor, and decide for yourself. I understand the kids sticking with their parents. I still love them all.

I feel at peace now. I don't miss all the drama. I hope my nieces will realize, in time that the battles I fought on my mother's behalf, were in *her* best interest, *always. I know I did nothing wrong.* I'm not working, but I'm surviving. My medical problems are stable and the medicines continue to work very well. I love my dog, and having him in my life has got me out of the house, and I have made many new friends. Both canine and human.

The drive across this beautiful country was once again a saving grace for me. I see God's work, so clearly in the natural world. Once again the people that I met on the road were very good to me. I met some very nice people. We took this trip leading up to the 2008 presidential election, and my bumper stickers were a good conversation starter. Even eliciting reactions from fellow travelers on the road. I don't know if I will ever have the chance to do it again. But, if I do, maybe on a motorcycle with a sidecar, or in a convertible. Just me and my best friend, Brody. ☺

Gary P. Stockbridge

OCTOBER IN WYOMING

Birthday list of all my nieces and nephews

        Noelle - January 21

        Gabrielle – February 20

        Leah – March 9

        Kate – March 24

        Shannon – March 28

        Jalyn – March 26

        Zachary – April 10

        Ma – April 24 *Rest in peace*

        Sarah – May 12

        Cassie – June 7

        Raisa – June 14

        Cristen – June 27

        Matthew – July 10

        Joshua – July 15

        Caleb – July 21

        Ashley – August 6

        Michael – August 14

        Cortney – September 13

        Jessie – September 16

        Alayne – November 10

        Robert – December 7

        Jarod James – December 9

Welcome to the newest additions
Faith and Lyla, and Amaya Linda

Thank You American Veterans